peaceful mind

Using Mindfulness & Cognitive Behavioral Psychology to Overcome Depression

JOHN R. MCQUAID, PH.D.
AND PAULA E. CARMONA, RN, MSN

Foreword by ZINDEL V. SEGAL, PH.D.

New Harbinger Publications, Inc.

Publisher's Note

This publication is designed to provide accurate and authoritative information in regard to the subject matter covered. It is sold with the understanding that the publisher is not engaged in rendering psychological, financial, legal, or other professional services. If expert assistance or counseling is needed, the services of a competent professional should be sought.

Distributed in Canada by Raincoast Books

Copyright © 2004 by John R. McQuaid, and Paula E. Carmona
New Harbinger Publications, Inc.
5674 Shattuck Avenue
Oakland, CA 94609

Cover design by Amy Shoup
Edited by Carole Honeychurch
Text design by Tracy Powell-Carlson

ISBN 1-57224-366-X Paperback

Printed in the United States of America

New Harbinger Publications' Web site address: www.newharbinger.com

06   05   04

10   9   8   7   6   5   4   3   2   1

First printing

Contents

foreword to *peaceful mind*

An important development in the psychological treatment of mood disorders has been the integration of mindfulness meditation and cognitive-behavioral psychology. By drawing on both these disciplines, people suffering from depression now have new tools for managing their mood problems. *Peaceful Mind* describes in a clear manner how to practically apply these tools in daily life.

Peaceful Mind suggests that mindful awareness and compassion towards oneself create the optimal platform for successful cognitive behavioral therapy. With clinical wisdom and an eye on the practical, McQuaid and Carmona introduce the basics of both. The authors themselves are well suited to the task and their collaboration emerges from a shared conviction in the possibility that depressed patients' lives can be improved by embracing the principles described herein. Each author contributes a unique skill set and perspective on depression treatment, one grounded in research on cognitive models of depression and the other reflecting a longstanding mindfulness practice and interest in Zen. Together they offer a compelling description of an integrative cognitive behavioral therapy broadened by its application across both the acute and recovery phases of depression and enlarged by its encounter with acceptance and mindfulness. Their approach allows for different points of entry into the work, depending on the stage at which people find themselves in dealing with their depression. Allowing some readers to merely dip a toe in the water while simultaneously supporting those who wish to plunge into the deep end is something this book does very well. This book is a patient-friendly user's guide to these exciting new developments.

—Zindel Segal, Ph.D.

acknowledgements

I would like to thank Sarah McQuaid for her support and encouragement throughout this project. I would also like to acknowledge my teachers and mentors, particularly Ricardo Muñoz, whose ideas about the healthy management of reality provided inspiration for this book.

—John R. McQuaid

I am grateful to the generous support of my husband, Fred Conway, for his fine editorial skills and unwavering big-heartedness as he accompanied me through this project. He held my heart and took care of the children with consistent selflessness.

I am deeply appreciative of the teachers at the San Diego Zen Center: of Charlotte Joko Beck for her incredible commitment to be as clear as possible and to teach her students as much as possible; of Elizabeth Hamilton for her embodiment of open heartedness and unflagging honesty; of Ezra Bayda for his clear articulation of practice. I am grateful to the many students at the Zen Center who have shared the practice of sitting together for so many years. They, too, have been my teachers.

I have much gratitude for my dear friend and colleague, Alby Quinlan, who provided insightful suggestions, editorial aid, and sustaining support along the way. Pat Ostrow used a wonderfully detailed editorial eye and a bounty of mindfulness as she read through several chapters. Dean Hill provided regular encouragement through his honest feedback and assessments of the work in progress. Barbara Thomson nurtured the creative spark and supported me through difficult hours.

I would also like to acknowledge my first teacher of meditation, my high school Spanish teacher, Bob King. He has been a lifelong friend whose grand and zany spirit has been a source of inspiration for many years. I hope his generous heart can be felt in *Peaceful Mind.*

—Paula E. Carmona

We are grateful to the San Diego Veterans Administration Healthcare System for being an institution that encourages the development of effective tools for helping people experiencing tough times. The development of programs in Mindfulness Based Stress Reduction, Dialectical Behavioral Therapy, and the Cognitive Behavioral Intervention Program has provided the institutional framework for the evolution of the ideas presented in *Peaceful Mind.* We appreciate the research conducted by Wiveka Ramel on mindfulness and depression, as this research catalyzed our collaboration on this book. We appreciate the many clients with whom we have worked who have taught us so much about the treatment of depression.

We would like to thank Catherine Sutker at New Harbinger's Publications who guided us through the process of writing this book. Carole Honeychurch was a delightful editor. Her ability to pay attention to the details of each sentence while holding the organization of the larger book in her mind is inspiring.

introduction

The motivation to write this book certainly comes from the desire to help the many people we have seen suffering from depression. But this is not just a book about getting rid of your depression. Our more earnest hope is to give you tools to help you transform your life. Transformation doesn't happen by merely getting rid of a problem. Transformation occurs when you have the capacity to greet the problems in your life with an open awareness and a keen interest. Learning how to be open to life and face painful problems is at the heart of our interest in exploring how mindfulness and cognitive behavioral therapy can be tools of transformation. A life shaken by depression is also a life open to the possibility of deep transformation. We hope that this book provides a useful foundation and skillful means to help you move beyond a life where depression is your shadow.

Our collaboration on *Peaceful Mind* comes from our mutual interest in treating the veterans at the San Diego Veterans Administration Healthcare System using the most optimal tools to change their lives. John is a psychologist who heads the Cognitive Behavioral Therapy Intervention Program at the V.A. He supervises interns and residents, does psychotherapy, and is active in his own research. Paula is a Psychiatric Clinical Nurse Specialist who has worked in mental health for seventeen years. Her interest in Zen meditation practice began in the early 70s. She has studied with Zen teacher and author Charlotte Joko Beck since 1984.

The authors first started working together when one of John's students, Wiveka Ramel, wanted to do research with the veterans who were enrolled in the Mindfulness Based Stress Reduction Program that Paula was teaching. The stress reduction program is an eight-week intensive program that introduces people to mindfulness meditation, yoga, and body scanning (a systematic way of developing awareness of sensations throughout the body). The initial research conducted by Ms. Ramel looked at how the practice of meditation influenced depressive symptoms. She found that the meditation helped reduce depressive symptoms and improve social functioning, which was consistent with previous findings by Jon Kabat-Zinn and his colleagues (Ramel and McQuaid 2001). Furthermore, she found that meditation could help some patients learn to control their attention so that they could pay more attention to positive stimuli and ignore negative stimuli, a potentially important factor in treating depression. The research also suggested that rumination (going over and over things in your mind that can make you feel depressed or anxious) decreased with mindfulness meditation practice. We were excited by these research results and began to discuss how mindfulness meditation could be integrated into the treatment of depression.

In 1998 we collaborated with our colleagues in the Veteran's Mental Health Clinic to implement a dialectical behavioral therapy (DBT) program to treat patients with borderline personality disorder, long considered one of the toughest problems in mental health. This model of treatment, developed by Marsha Linehan, Ph.D., integrates mindfulness with a well-designed cognitive behavioral therapy program. We have been deeply impressed with the powerful influence that this program had in lessening symptoms and reducing the need for hospitalization.

When we decided to take on the challenge of writing this book we believed that we could bring a useful combination of our knowledge and experience to bear on the project. Paula could contribute her real-life practice with mindfulness meditation, teaching stress reduction, and dialectical behavioral therapy, and John could contribute expertise from his years of teaching, researching, and providing cognitive behavioral therapy. It is our hope that this book will provide guidance so you can understand how to use mindfulness and cognitive behavioral therapy to transform the suffering of depression into a deeply satisfying life.

Thoughts on How to Use
Peaceful Mind

People read books differently depending on where they are in their lives. Some people who read this book might be starting to explore whether they have a serious problem with depression, whereas others might have successfully overcome a period of depression and want to learn new ways to deal with their depression should it recur. Where you are in your life, and more specifically how you relate to issues regarding depression, will to some extent determine how you might want to approach reading *Peaceful Mind*. Some folks may be eager to try everything in the book, and other people may just want to read the book and gather information. One of the reasons people use books differently is that they are in different stages of change. The concept of stages of change basically is that people who have problems that could benefit from help tend to go through a series of stages in recognizing the problem, deciding to do something, and then actually taking action to fix the problem (Prochaska, Norcross, and DiClemente 1994). What things are most helpful to you in dealing with the problem depend on your current stage of change. We would like to use some of the lessons learned from the stages of change philosophy to provide some suggestions on how you might consider using this book.

An Overview of Change

The first two stages of change are called *precontemplation* and *contemplation*. In these two stages you are working toward acknowledging that you have a mood problem. If you have picked up this book because you're wondering if you are depressed or someone close to you has expressed concern about your poor mood, you could be in the precontemplation stage of change. If you believe you are depressed, and you're not sure what you want to do about it, you may be in the contemplation stage of change. It's very important in either stage of change to just clearly see what's going on with you at this time and not be critical of yourself. If you think you might be in either of these two stages, we would advise you to read through the book to obtain new information or learn how to look at your problems from a new angle. We would not recommend that you try to do all the exercises or new skills in this book immediately. However, we would encourage you to try to learn more about yourself using the mindfulness skills. As you move from the contemplation to the *action* stage of change (where you have decided to do something to deal with your depression), you would benefit from trying some of the activities to "road test" whether the new behaviors benefit you. If you find that you're strongly resistant to doing new activities, then this is probably not the right time to take that on. We would encourage you to just read the book. If, on the other hand, you feel even slightly motivated to change your life, we would suggest that you commit yourself to doing all the exercises in the book. Give yourself some time each day to read and do the activities. Pay close attention to the lessons coming up about how to evaluate the effectiveness of those activities. If you are in the last two stages of change, *maintenance* and *termination,* we would suggest that you focus your attention on what is problematic in your life now, and challenge yourself with taking on the mindfulness and cognitive behavioral skills that would enrich your life.

Thoughts on the Organization of *Peaceful Mind*

We have organized the book to initially give you broad overviews and then offer more specific help. In chapter 1 there is a discussion of the symptoms of depression and a brief overview of mindfulness and cognitive behavioral therapy. We also discuss the research on depression that has influenced our decision to combine mindfulness and cognitive psychology. Chapter 2, "The Combo Plate," further examines the overlap between these two fields and how the integration of mindfulness and cognitive behavioral therapy might benefit someone who may be depressed. In chapter 2 we introduce the powerful role that observation has in mindfulness and cognitive behavioral therapy. In this chapter we begin to look at how "muscle of awareness" develops from a mindfulness practice.

We then move to more practical specifics. In chapter 3, "First Steps," we focus more on the skills and approaches that you can begin to use to help your depression.

The powerful influence of core beliefs (the guiding theme for this book) is detailed in chapter 4. In this chapter we explain the framework for your core-belief structure. We look at the supporting framework of assumptions, strategies, and automatic thoughts. We introduce a powerful technique used in cognitive therapy called the downward arrow, and discuss an important aspect of mindfulness practice, how to notice your thoughts.

Chapters 5 through 8 are the main chapters where we describe how to start using the major tools of cognitive therapy to work effectively toward relief from depression. Mindfulness is interwoven into these skills to support greater awareness and the effective use of the skills. Chapter 5 helps the reader understand the limitations of depressed thinking and learn how to catch, check, and change thoughts. How to move beyond the inertia created by depression by engaging in activities is the focus of chapter 6. Chapters 7 and 8 are the "people" chapters. In chapter 7 we look at the all-important role of how the quality of relationships you have with others influences your depression. Through case examples we look at how these relationships are influenced by core beliefs. In chapter 8 we discuss how to improve your communication skills. Throughout this set of chapters we offer you a variety of new skills and exercises to practice.

In chapter 9 we provide guidelines on how to include physical exercise in your daily routine to help you combat depression. We provide examples of how you can incorporate skills from cognitive behavioral therapy and mindfulness to have success with an exercise program.

"Acceptance is Not Defeat" is the title for chapter 10. In this chapter we explore how a change in perspective can be a remarkable agent to help people acknowledge the problems in their life, without getting tied up in knots over those problems. We use mindfulness and skills from dialectical behavioral therapy to demonstrate how healing acceptance can be possible.

The final chapter, "Stages of Change," integrates mindfulness and cognitive behavioral skills with the stages-of-change model. We explore how these skills can be applied at different stages of change. We hope that this approach will help you fine tune the skills you have learned by reading *Peaceful Mind* and let you apply them to your life so that you have the greatest possibility of wisely integrating mindfulness and cognitive behavioral therapy into your daily life.

As we move now into an explanation of depression and how mindfulness and cognitive therapy can be of help, consider watching your responses to the information provided. These responses will be the beginning steps of mindfulness and will help you consider what stage of change you are in.

1

from depression to hope

Peaceful Pathways

If you have struggled with depression, a peaceful mind and a light heart can seem like an elusive dream. Depression slips the mind into a dark state where even the hope of better days becomes hard to imagine. This lack of hope is not accurate, however. Hope is possible because there are pathways to move out of depression, and there are tools that can be used to help you along the path. You can move from this dark state of depression to a place of contentment through knowledge and steady effort. This book can provide you with the skills you need to know to find your path away from the pain of depression and the tools to keep you on the path. We will give you guidance so you can gain insight into yourself and tools to help you use your insights to reach a life of deeper satisfaction.

Remember when you were in school and learned a new skill? Whether it was writing in cursive, learning your multiplication tables, writing a term paper, or designing a science experiment, you had to do something you may not have been confident you could do. But somehow you got through it and acquired knowledge, new skills, and maybe even self-confidence. While we're not taking you back to school, we do intend to challenge you with new ideas. You will be shown new skills, asked to design experiments, look at your mood patterns, and discover your core beliefs that contribute to depression. If you're currently depressed you may not believe you can do anything right now. Depression takes away confidence, seeming to sap it right out of your bones. Even if you are feeling desiccated, like a dried bag of bones and ready to let the next strong wind blow you to the nearest town, take this moment to learn about the possibilities that are on the horizon.

On the horizon is a new integration of the basics of cognitive behavioral therapy with mindfulness meditation. From this synthesis we hope to distill what will be most helpful to someone struggling with a blue mood or even a clinical depressive disorder. We will be presenting an overview of both cognitive behavioral therapy and mindfulness approaches to help you sort out your problems and learn ways to improve your mood.

But this book is not solely about learning how to overcome your problems by just doing things differently. Beyond external skills, we believe that you can learn how to go inside yourself and clearly see your thoughts and emotions, also feeling present with your physical self from a place of just being, not trying to change anything. We believe that learning these skills of being with yourself in an accepting, nonjudgmental way can both help end depression and lead to a more deeply gratifying life. From these experiences of being, using your open heart and perceptive mind, you will be able to develop new skills in relating to yourself and the life around you, creating a fulfilling life without depression.

The Experience of Depression

The word depression is used to describe many states, including brief drops in mood, stretches of sadness, or an ongoing feeling of melancholy. However, when we refer to depression, we are referring to an emotional disorder that disrupts your emotions as well as your thinking, actions, and body.

Depression shows itself in many ways. For some, depression is the struggle to get out of bed in the morning after a night of watching the clock. You might know the feeling of your mind turning to mush. Perhaps you had a mind that was once quite active and skillful in your area of expertise, and you watched that mind become incapacitated, unable to move out of the stupor of darkness and anguish of despair. At one time you could remember details, but now you're so depressed that you can't even recall some basic facts for your work. For many, hopelessness is a powerful part of depression. It washes over you, and you simply don't know what to do. You know you have mental pain, but it doesn't make sense to you that your whole body aches and that you feel disconnected from your body. You wonder where you'll ever get the will to change. Your mind is gnarled up with thoughts of self-condemnation. The funnel of gloom draws you downward, and you feel extraordinarily guilty, like somehow you did something terrible and you *deserve* to reside in this place of depression.

This is depression; it is dark, deep, and dangerous. It can lead to suicidal thoughts and even suicide attempts. If you are depressed, there is hope, and there is recovery from depression. The following is an explanation about how depressive disorders are defined by mental health professionals.

How Depression is Defined Clinically

Mental-health clinicians use a book called *The Diagnostic and Statistical Manual of Mental Disorders, Fourth Edition* (or *DSM-IV*, for short) to define conditions such as depression (American Psychiatric Association 2000). The *DSM-IV* defines three types of depressive disorder that this book is designed to address. They are major depression, minor depression, and dysthymia.

Major depression and minor depression are diagnosed when a person suffers from several of the following nine symptoms:

✦ Feeling sad

✦ Not enjoying things you used to find pleasurable

✦ Being either slower than usual, or being more agitated

✦ Having low energy

✦ Having trouble sleeping (either too much or too little)

✦ Having trouble eating (either too much or too little)

✦ Experiencing guilt, worthlessness, or hopelessness

✦ Having trouble concentrating

✦ Thinking a great deal about death

Major Depression

Major depression is a serious mood disorder in which you have at least five of the symptoms nearly all day, every day, for at least two weeks. The five symptoms must include either sadness or decreased enjoyment. The average episode of major depression lasts six months, and some episodes can last years. Major depression tends to recur. If you have one episode, you have a 50 to 80 percent chance of a second episode (Judd 1997).

Minor Depression

Minor depression is similar to major depression, but with fewer symptoms. It has only recently been included as a diagnostic disorder in the *DSM-IV* and is listed as a preliminary diagnosis that is being researched. According to the *DSM-IV*, you are having an episode of minor depression if you show any two to four of the nine symptoms nearly all day, every day, for at least two weeks. Minor depression can lead to trouble functioning, and it is a risk factor for major depression. Treatment of minor depression may prevent the development of major depression.

Dysthymia

Dysthymia is not as well-known a term as depression, but it's a fairly common condition. The symptoms of dysthymia tend to be less severe than those of depression (occurring most days but not every day) while lasting longer (at least two years). People with dysthymia suffer at least two of the following symptoms:

✦ Poor appetite or overeating

✦ Decreased or too much sleep

✦ Low energy or fatigue

✦ Low self-esteem

✦ Poor concentration or indecisiveness

✦ Hopelessness

Times to Seek Immediate Help

If your depressive symptoms are so severe that you're having trouble taking care of yourself or getting through the day, it's important that you get additional help from a professional who treats emotional problems. Examples of severe depressive symptoms are:

✦ You can't get out of bed and are no longer eating or taking care of your basic needs.

✦ You think about hurting yourself.

✦ You think about hurting others.

There are many effective treatments for mood problems, including psychotherapy and medication. In the appendix we provide some suggestions on how you can get further help.

Bipolar Disorder

There is a class of mood disorders, called bipolar disorders, which this book is not designed to treat. People with bipolar disorders cycle between depressive symptoms, like those listed above, and manic symptoms, which are listed below:

✦ Feeling extremely good about yourself

✦ Doing risky, impulsive things like spending or traveling

✦ Speaking much faster than usual

✦ Having high energy

✦ Needing much less sleep

✦ Being easily distracted

✦ Increased goal-directed behavior

✦ Thinking so fast you cannot keep your ideas straight

While psychotherapy can be helpful for bipolar disorder, the most effective treatment is medication, and there are several effective medications available. If you think you have symptoms of mania and are not receiving treatment, it is very important to speak with a psychiatrist and be evaluated for treatment.

If you're suffering from the symptoms of major depression, minor depression, or dysthymia, this book is designed to help you. Even if you don't have any of these diagnostic disorders on an ongoing basis, struggling only at times with a poor mood, you can benefit from learning the skills of CBT and mindfulness. We hope that you find that the skills of CBT and mindfulness can help you with a blue mood and can aid you in your everyday life to realize a new level of self-knowledge and satisfaction.

Mindfulness: A Brief Overview

We use the word "mindfulness" in this book to mean moment-to-moment awareness. It is learning to wake up to each moment of your life so that you are fully living your life in this moment. Mindfulness is a part of all the major religious traditions. Mindfulness meditation has its origins in Buddhist traditions in Asia and has now been assimilated into the Western world through many venues. You can practice mindfulness regardless of your own religious background or personal beliefs in God. Mindfulness is not a mysterious mystical state; rather, it is being fully aware of the reality around you. Mindfulness is maintaining awareness of the sensations in your body, the flow of thoughts through your mind, the sounds and sights in your surroundings. Thus, mindfulness is awareness expanded into ourselves and outward into the world.

People cultivate mindfulness by learning to consciously place their attention on whatever is happening moment by moment. Many people start to learn mindfulness on a formal basis by developing a meditation practice. Meditation is a powerful pathway to learning mindfulness, but it is not the only pathway. Some people come to mindfulness through a conscious exercise program, others by having a daily ritual, a hobby, or a place of honest reflection. However someone comes to mindfulness, there are usually shared experiences for those who are on this path.

The foundation that supports all mindfulness practice is experiencing life without judging it. This quality of mind is usually referred to as "nonjudgmental awareness." Nonjudgmental awareness does not mean that you cease to have judgmental thoughts. Rather, you begin to learn to question whether those judgments are indeed facts.

It is from this place of nonjudgmental awareness that you can allow yourself to open to all that is within you and be more conscious of all that surrounds you. We will be exploring both how you can develop a mindfulness practice and the advantages of living a life where mindfulness informs your awareness. It is our experience that people who develop mindfulness in their lives develop a more gentle and honest relationship with themselves, and this is infinitely helpful if you are feeling depressed.

Cognitive Behavioral Therapy: A Brief Overview

Whereas mindfulness comes from an Eastern tradition more than 2500 years old, the roots of cognitive therapy and cognitive behavioral therapy extend back 2500 years in the Western tradition, to the time of Socrates. This is when philosophers initially described the use of logic and rationality to question assumptions. Aaron Beck and his colleagues particularly cite the work of the stoic philosophers of the fourth century B.C., who proposed that emotions arose from ideas (Beck et al. 1979). The development of cognitive therapy as a treatment for depression is generally credited to Aaron T. Beck, who described this approach in the 1960s.

Cognitive therapy is based on a simple premise: your emotional response to a situation is due to how you think about that situation. "Cognitive" means related to thinking. Some types of thinking are more likely to lead to feeling depressed in certain situations. These types of thinking tend to be inaccurate, or distortions of what is really going on. By learning to notice the depressive thoughts and question their accuracy, you can then generate new, more accurate thoughts that lead to a better mood.

You might notice that the last two paragraphs refer to cognitive therapy, while the section heading refers to cognitive behavioral therapy. That is because the model that Dr. Beck originally created was cognitive therapy. While Dr. Beck pointed out that behaviors (activities) were also important, his emphasis was most strongly focused on retraining thinking. However, several other researchers emphasized the role of pleasant and rewarding activities in helping people overcome depression, and in the model we present we focus on both thinking and activities. Therefore, we are going to call this cognitive behavioral therapy, or CBT for short.

There are a couple of other important points to know about CBT. There are several assumptions about how you end up at the point where your thinking is making you depressed. First, we assume that how you think and what you do is learned, based on the principle that you will do something more often if it leads to some reward or prevents some punishment. For example, if you tend to criticize yourself a lot (which is pretty common in depression), doing so probably was an effective thing to do sometime in your life. Maybe by criticizing yourself, you avoided other people criticizing you. Maybe your own criticism drove you to succeed.

Whatever the reason, this type of thinking worked then. General, overarching themes in your thinking like these are called your "core beliefs."

However, if you are currently depressed, those core beliefs you learned in the past are no longer working to your benefit. It may be that you're in a different place in life, or maybe you are facing a particular challenge or life event where your old core beliefs don't work, but rather lead to depression. These assumptions upon which CBT is based have three important implications for dealing with your depression. First, you are not crazy for being depressed or thinking and acting the way you do when you're depressed. You think and act the way you do because it made sense at some point in your life, and sometimes the world around us changes faster than we do. Second, it doesn't necessarily matter how you learned to think this way, it just matters whether this way of thinking works for you now in your current life. If it's not working, it is time to change how you think and what you do. Third, because you learned to think and act the way you do, you can learn to think and act in a different way. Learning new things uses the same principles you used to learn your old ways; you actually do the new things and see if they lead to rewards (like better moods) or avoid punishments (like bad moods).

Given these principles, CBT employs the following steps. First you learn to observe your thoughts, actions, and feelings and see how they influence each other. You then identify those thoughts and actions that seem to cause you to feel more depressed and learn to check them out. You question whether the thoughts are true and accurate or whether they actually mislead you and increase your depression. You check whether your activities are making you feel worse and whether you might be able to do different activities that improve your mood. Next, you experiment with new thoughts and new activities. You develop new, more accurate thoughts based on the evidence you see around you, and check to see if these thoughts lead to a better mood. You try doing old activities differently or try new activities, and see if these improve your mood.

What people often find is that thinking and acting in a new way feels difficult, uncomfortable, and even unnatural at first. This makes perfect sense since you're changing things that you've probably done for a long time. In fact, it is a good sign if things seem very different when you start, since the old way of doing things wasn't working. As you move through a course of CBT, the new ways become more automatic, and you become more skilled. When you end a course of CBT, you have a new set of thoughts and actions as well as the ability to adjust to new challenges.

Is This Worth Trying?

The techniques in this book have been studied in a variety of ways to determine whether they are beneficial. The following is a brief review of the research on CBT and mindfulness in the treatment of depression. A number of studies have examined whether CBT reduces depression. In addition, some studies have tested whether CBT reduces the risk of further episodes of depression and improves response to medication. Finally, there are a few recent studies that have examined whether mindfulness and CBT together are effective in treating mental health problems.

CBT Reduces Depression

Many studies have shown that CBT reduces depression. Aaron T. Beck and his colleagues, who initially developed CBT, completed a trial in which they compared CBT to the standard medication for depression. They found that CBT was more effective at reducing depression (Rush et al. 1977). Several additional studies found similar results (see Dobson, 1989, for a review of studies of CBT for depression). One major study, however, found that CBT, unlike medication and intepersonal psychotherapy (IPT, another psychotherapy for depression), was not significantly better then placebo (Elkin 1989). On the other hand, this same study found that there were not significant differences in the effect of CBT, medication, and IPT. Despite this one result, researchers continued to compare CBT and other treatments. Subsequent studies generally found CBT to be superior to placebo and not significantly different from medications and IPT. In the final analysis, CBT is considered to have strong evidence that it works for depression (DeRubeis and Crits-Cristoph 1998).

The skills learned in CBT can be beneficial in a broad range of life experiences, not just managing your mood. And experiencing recovery from depression based on your own actions can give you a strong sense of accomplishment when contrasted with treatment by medication alone. Finally, as noted below, there is evidence that treatment by CBT may have longer-term benefits than medication.

CBT Reduces Risk for Relapse

CBT has been found to reduce the risk of future episodes of depression when compared to treatment by medication. Research suggests that individuals who complete a course of CBT have a reduced risk of relapse compared to those who respond to medication and then discontinue their medication (Simons, Murphy, and Wetzel 1986). These authors suggest that this may be due to the skills learned in CBT providing you with the ability to cope more effectively with challenges that otherwise would have led to depression.

Combined Treatment: Medication and CBT

Many researchers have expressed interest in combining medication and CBT, hoping that the combination would be more effective than either one alone. Interestingly, this has generally not been the case. In most studies, combined treatment has been only slightly more effective than either medication or CBT alone (Hollon et al. 1992). However, there is one important exception to this. A large study of patients with chronic depression (either dysthymia or at least two years of major depression) compared medication (nefazadone), a version of CBT, and the two combined (Keller et al. 2000). Whereas about 50 percent of the patients in either of the single treatments got better, 80 percent in the combined treatment got better. There are a couple of things to notice about this study. First, since it focused on people with chronic depression, it may suggest that these people are the ones most likely to benefit from combined treatment. Second, the study used a modified type of CBT that emphasized understanding core beliefs and interactions with people. It may be that chronic depression benefits particularly from attention to core beliefs and interpersonal interactions. Another combined treatment study took a different approach. Giovanni Fava and his colleagues tested whether CBT could be added after successful medication treatment (Fava et al. 1998). He assigned patients who had been treated with medication and recovered from their depression to two different experimental groups. The first group received eight weeks of CBT that was designed to promote happy living. The second group was the control group and got no additional treatment. Both groups were tapered off their medication (that is, they slowly reduced their medication doses until they stopped taking medication). After two years, the group without treatment was three times more likely to have become depressed again compared to the CBT group.

These studies suggest that medication and CBT can work together in a complementary manner. If you are currently taking medication, please continue to use it as instructed by the person who prescribed it. It's probably a good idea to tell your medication provider if you decide to use this book so that you can work together to manage your depression.

Mindfulness and CBT

Several recent CBT models have incorporated mindfulness techniques. Different studies use different labels, but a shared component of the approaches that we will refer to as mindfulness is the nonjudgmental observation of your own internal experience.

Two particular sets of studies have influenced us. The first were those of Marsha Linehan and her colleagues. She argued that patients with borderline personality disorder, for whom their treatment is intended, have great difficulty in tolerating painful emotions and few skills with which to change those emotions. This model includes extensive training in techniques of observing, making nonjudgmental descriptions of experience, and learning to tolerate distress. In addition, the program teaches patients how to deal with people more effectively and how to change behaviors that are self-destructive. The central theme to this approach was balancing mindful awareness with effective behavior change.

Linehan's treatment for borderline personality disorder was the first to be compared to a control condition (a group of patients who did not receive Linehan's treatment), and it proved to be effective at reducing suicide attempts and self-destructive behavior (Linehan et al. 1991). This has now been replicated in another study that also found that this treatment reduced depressed symptoms and misery.

The second set of studies that have influenced us come from the work of Zindel Segal, Mark Williams, John Teasdale, and their research groups. These researchers were studying depression from several different but related perspectives when they developed an interest in how the techniques of mindfulness meditation might be related to the effective ingredients in CBT. They started to study mindfulness meditation, as described by Jon Kabat-Zinn in his book *Full-Catastrophe Living* (1990). Based on their extensive research in cognitive processes in depression, these authors developed a model of what they call "maintenance CBT" to prevent the relapse of depression after treatment with medication. This model integrated mindfulness exercises with cognitive therapy. The treatment provides the patient with skills to be able to observe their own thoughts and feelings without becoming too wrapped up in them. Basically, you learn that a thought is just a thought, and that you always have a choice or not to react to that thought. In a study of this approach, the researchers compared two groups of patients who had been depressed but had responded to medication and were not currently depressed (Teasdale et al. 2000). Patients got either eight weeks of the mindfulness-based cognitive therapy (MBCT) or normal treatment (which means doing whatever they would usually do). They found that patients with three or more previous episodes of depression were less likely to relapse if they received MBCT.

Creating Your Own Experiment

All these findings we've reviewed are promising and led us to write this book. In designing the interventions we present here, we have drawn as much as possible on treatments that are firmly backed by research evidence. However, the specific model presented here has not been tested in a randomized, placebo-controlled study (the scientific standard for figuring out if a treatment works). Therefore, we encourage anyone using this book to look at it like a scientist and think about it as an experiment, where you're testing whether the techniques you learn are useful for you. As you go through the book, we will give you specific ideas on how to test out the skills you are learning. After a while, you will probably have acquired several skills that you find are helpful and will notice other suggestions are not as helpful. We hope you can use the things you learn to develop a personal plan for managing your mood and creating the life you want.

2

the combo plate

Two for One: CBT and Mindfulness

When you go out to a restaurant do you sometimes want the combination plate? Do you think, "I'd like to taste both the tamale and the enchilada?" Like the combo plate where you taste different flavors, combining mindfulness and CBT brings together different traditions and theoretical backgrounds that help people lead a more meaningful, connected, and productive life. They are both mind-body approaches to living a more fulfilling life. In other words, both approaches help people notice and understand how physical feelings, emotions, and thoughts are related and interact. For the depressed person, the hope for a life that holds meaning and fulfillment seems remote, as they cannot see their way out of the darkness. In this chapter we offer guidance about how you can use knowledge from the spiritual and the psychological to find your way back into a life with light, a life worth living.

The Combination Advantage

What are the advantages of combining the tools of meditation and cognitive therapy in the treatment of depression? The most fundamental advantage is that, when woven together, the skills of self-observation are mutually enhanced, like threads woven together to eventually become a fabric that is stronger, more durable, and reliable than the threads alone. When self-knowledge is gained though different intellectual, spiritual, physical, and emotional means, it is inherently stronger than a narrow approach, where you only get to experience and know a limited aspect of yourself.

Mindfulness and CBT together provide you with a broader, more comprehensive process for treating your depressive symptoms. Mindfulness fosters self-knowledge by helping you be present to your flow of thoughts and sensations, moment by moment. Because you don't have to necessarily do anything with what you observe, there is a type of permission you grant to yourself to just watch the good, bad, and ugly move right through you. This open awareness provides an observational strategy that helps you move deep into yourself.

CBT has a comprehensive organization that provides you with skills to make changes. Sometimes what is learned from your mindfulness will inform the work you will want to do using the techniques of CBT. This can also be a reciprocal relationship, where you'll learn things about yourself in CBT and learn to "sit" with these aspects of yourself in your mindfulness practice. This "sitting with" practice is the foundation for developing distress tolerance and compassionate awareness, which will be elaborated on further in the book.

Typically, when you start either meditation or cognitive therapy you are engaging in a process of getting to know yourself. People usually start cognitive therapy because something is wrong; they are depressed, anxious, afraid, panicked, or just plain worried. More often than not, people also start meditation because they feel something is wrong. There is a feeling of unease, discontent, and perhaps spiritual emptiness. Whether the starting point is because of a diagnosable psychiatric problem or general malaise, the first goal of both meditation and cognitive therapy is to get to know yourself.

What do we mean by getting to know yourself? In the language used in CBT, you learn to track your thoughts, to observe your behaviors, and to notice how the thoughts and behaviors affect your emotions, especially your depressed mood. Furthermore, CBT guides you to look at your activities and relationships with people to help you consider how these influence your sense of self. In the language of mindfulness meditation, you learn to observe the mind, label and describe thoughts, experience sensations, and reside in the present moment. In either case, you become intimate with the daily flow of both casual and deeply believed thoughts. Through these self-observational strategies you learn to notice how your behavior, thoughts, and sensations are influenced by your core beliefs system, which is introduced later in this chapter and explored thoroughly in chapter 4.

Ways of Seeing: CBT

Cognitive therapy has a ready-made framework that is designed to treat depression in a structured, organized, and linear manner. It is designed to help people learn about themselves by using the rational part of their brain to observe their thoughts, emotions, moods, and behavior. The first step in cognitive therapy is learning to recognize that the types of thoughts we think clearly affect our mood. The insidious power of negative thoughts is not to be underestimated, as negative thoughts are often sly, hiding from everyday awareness while influencing beliefs and actions. CBT can often be a great eye-opener for people to become aware of the depth, subtlety, persistence, and tenacity of these negative thoughts.

In cognitive therapy, thoughts that occur during a depressed mood are closely examined to discover if they are accurate or false, to see if they promote or deter a depressed mood. To illustrate this point, consider the example of Bob, a fictional case we will use as an example throughout this book. How do you think the thoughts that run through Bob's head one evening might make him feel?

Bob is a forty-three-year-old married, employed white man who is feeling down. When he gets home after work, he realizes he forgot to pick up food for dinner, even though his wife Mary had called and asked him to just before he left. Bob thinks, "I'm an idiot. I can't even remember something for fifteen minutes. Mary is really going to be angry!"

Understandably, Bob feels pretty lousy after silently berating himself. But rather than just believing the negative thought, "I'm an idiot," the depressed person using CBT skills first develops the awareness that this is only a thought, and furthermore, that thoughts are often not accurate. If Bob is aware of his thoughts, he can question them:

✦ Does forgetting something make him an idiot?

✦ Are there any other reasons he might forget besides being an idiot?

✦ Would he be as critical of someone he cares about?

✦ How often does Mary get "really angry?"

✦ Is it possible that Mary might understand?

✦ If she really does get angry, is that the end of the world?

Cognitive therapy directly examines thoughts and trains people to challenge thoughts that are inaccurate and to recognize how their thoughts influence their mood and behavior. Like a lawyer, a person using cognitive therapy will tenaciously pursue evidence for and against the depressive thought. Teaching yourself to poke holes in your negative thoughts is a key strategy to shifting your depressed mood. Useful questions that can help you challenge your unhelpful thoughts include the following:

✦ Is this thought accurate?

✦ When has this thought not been true?

✦ What makes me think this thought is true now?

✦ What makes me think this thought is false now?

As you learn more about your daily thinking and functioning we encourage you to write down your thoughts, moods, and behavior in a journal or notebook. This recording is *very* important because it helps you to:

✦ Develop the capacity to watch yourself and learn about the patterns of your thinking

✦ Recognize thoughts to be challenged

✦ Recognize and measure change in your depression

✦ Take the knowledge from this book into the real world by practicing what you read

Self-observation also helps you track the relationship between your activity level and your depression. Behavior theory tells us that if you increase your rewarding activities you increase the likelihood that your depression will decrease. If you get out of bed when you wake up and go for a thirty-minute walk you will probably feel better than if you stayed in bed for thirty more minutes. In this book we ask you to track your level of depression in relationship to activities (such as exercise, going out with people, taking classes, going to work) so that these aspects of your life also become fair game in the evaluation and treatment of depression.

Beliefs behind Behavior

As you progress, one goal is to become aware of one or more core beliefs that drive your behavior. This is also a goal in an awareness-based meditation practice. A *core belief* is a strongly held belief about yourself or the world that drives your assumptions about yourself, the world, and the future. CBT suggests that core beliefs often develop early as children learn to cope in the world. However, such beliefs continue to be held, even if they cause problems like depression, because they are the foundation for the framework in which people think about their current experiences. In other words, people will naturally pay more attention to both the events in their everyday life and their internal thoughts that reinforce their core beliefs.

Consider now how Bob's core belief can make him vulnerable to feeling depressed. Bob's belief is "I'm not good enough." This belief leads him to be very anxious and avoid new activities.

CBT might teach Bob to remember a time he was successful and gather evidence that challenges the validity of the core belief. As he makes these challenges, Bob can notice himself coming up with new reasons why the success was an exception. He can then challenge these additional unhelpful thoughts. Bob might then try and devise an experiment that will further test the core belief, "I am not good enough." He may decide to take a class, or participate in an athletic activity to test the accuracy of this belief. Again, he uses the information gained from the experience to challenge the core belief system.

With cognitive therapy you learn to connect the automatic thoughts that occur in response to events or stimuli back to your core belief. As you progress you can design simple experiments to evaluate your automatic negative thoughts and thereby gather evidence to test the accuracy of your core belief.

A problem people encounter when they try to devise experiments to challenge their core beliefs is they have a thought like, "Well, I'm just trying to construct experiments to fool myself into denying the truth," because core beliefs feel so darn real and true. To experiment with shifting your core belief requires using mindfulness to first notice your resistance to change and then allowing yourself to move in a new direction, noting at each step of the way how your negative thoughts and probable physical discomfort makes it hard to get started. As you begin challenging your core belief it's likely you will need to let two seemingly opposite truths be observed simultaneously: one truth being your conviction about your core belief being true, and the other truth is that core beliefs are not always based in reality. With this broader perspective you can avoid the battle about whether your core belief is true or not, and simply use your open mind to delve into what is real in this moment.

All of these self-observational tools are important when people are working towards relief from depression. You can learn a tremendous amount about how you perceive yourself, how you process information, how you relate to others, and how all of this affects your level of depression. Overall, cognitive therapy provides a well-researched structure and therapeutic strategies for using self-awareness to relieve depression.

Ways of Seeing: Mindfulness Meditation

Cognitive therapy emphasizes trying to change the way you think. Meditation starts with simply observing the mind and body without necessarily trying to change what is seen or the seer. Most people come to meditation with the hope of changing their sense of self, but the inherent framework of a meditation practice is actually not geared towards self-improvement. Rather, meditation is more radically geared towards accepting life as it is. This capacity for accepting life starts with learning to sit quietly and observe what passes through the mind and body in a nonjudgmental fashion. Many teachers have described observing our mind as watching our thoughts go by like clouds passing in the broad sky. This metaphor helps us give permission to experience thoughts and emotions moving in and out of us, like clouds moving in the sky with no place for them to attach. When we give ourselves the permission to watch the natural phenomena of the mind and body, we come to directly experience the mind and body, thoughts and sensations, as constantly changing.

If you are depressed, you might not want to observe the content of your thinking. Some common thoughts about mindfulness include, "If I pay attention to my thoughts, I will just feel worse" or, "I can't just observe and notice my thinking; I want to change how I feel!" If you notice thoughts like these or any others making it hard to practice mindfulness, you can first give yourself credit for noticing the thoughts! What mindful observation can do is increase your understanding that your thoughts only have the power that you give them, and that we give thoughts power when we believe them unquestioningly. For example, if Bob says, "I'm an idiot," and believes it, he feels worse. If he says, "I'm an idiot" and just notices this without judging whether it's true, it becomes more of an object of interest and can lead to self-discovery. What led to that thought? How did he react to that thought? How did the thought affect his mood and physical sensations? This sequence of observation and awareness leads to greater choices in how to respond. It also, indirectly, makes the thought less disturbing, as we stop treating thoughts as unquestioned truths but rather as just things to observe.

Let's look at another example. One client we'll call Steve came to a session extremely upset. He had left another meeting because the person with whom he was speaking refused a request. Consequently he had a visual image of hitting the person. When he came to session, he was not only angry about the refusal but feeling horrible about the image.

At this point, it's important to consider that there are many ways Steve could have reacted to the image. While it may make sense to be upset, someone else might feel regret, another may feel anxious, and so on. The emotional response will depend on what they are telling themselves about having the image. Steve was telling himself, "I'm out of control. I have these images come into my mind, and that means I'm an a—hole who is going to hurt someone." This fit with his core belief that he was defective. However, if he takes a mindful approach, Steve will notice the image and not judge it. He won't assume that he will act on it or that it means anything horrible about him. He might notice what led to the image and how having the image affects him. But for now, it is just an image. When we tried this in therapy, Steve felt a great deal of relief and was able to recognize that just having an image did not mean he was going to do something terrible. In fact, he hadn't done anything terrible and had just walked away.

Developing the Muscle of Awareness

The layers of the mind are peeled away with meditation. We get to know our fears, our strategies for avoiding life, our preferred defenses, and our basic core beliefs. Self-observation is a skill. As with other skills, you practice to become competent. Like an athlete practicing their sport, the meditator practices developing the muscle of awareness. Awareness grows by repeated practice of observing thoughts and emotions passing through the mind and body. Our natural tendency is to have a thought and then think about the thought, judging it as a good, bad, or interesting. It takes a broad awareness to recognize these layers of thoughts: the original thought, the judgment about the thought, and then the thought about the judgment.

We are told that meditation is a practice of staying with or being in each moment as it arises. But often we really prefer to daydream, plan, think about the future, or in some way avoid being alert to what is going on right now. Over time we learn to observe what it is that we want to avoid and to physically feel the sensations that we previously tried to avoid. This tolerance or even willingness to reside mentally and physically in the body is part of the skill acquisition of an ongoing practice. Meditation does not then become a means of escape from the unpleasantness of life; rather, meditation is the vehicle to experience life directly, whether it is pleasant or unpleasant. In mindfulness meditation we do not try to escape to some blissful place—we stay with each moment. When we want to avoid staying with each moment, we notice that urge to avoid and literally sit with our avoidance. We carefully watch the thoughts that arise about not liking this moment. We feel the body resist this moment. As we stay with our resistance, we again exercise the muscle of awareness. However, building the muscle broadens the awareness. The awareness is no longer narrow and constricted; it is a wide awareness that allows us to be aware of our difficulties *and* of the broader environment: the sound in the room, the smell of the outdoors, and the sensation of the air against the skin. From this place of expanded awareness you can watch your thoughts and impulses change and fade. You can develop the internal stability to watch the movement of your mind, as though you were lying on a grassy field watching the thought-clouds move across the vast sky. This broad, open awareness trains you to be aware of difficulties but also provides mental and physical training for you not to be locked into your misery. This capacity to direct your attention is an important point in the treatment of depression.

The greater your capacity to direct your attention on areas of life that are supportive or life giving, the greater your capacity to positively transform a depressed mood. Through the repeated training of meditation, you develop the skills to turn the mind and attention toward health and away from self-destructive thoughts and habits.

A Spiritual Practice

This same muscle of awareness that we use to fight depression also gives us the capacity to taste life, change, and impermanence. Digging deep into yourself, you also dig deep into the nature of life and death. And meditation, more than most psychological therapies, gives you the mental and physical tools to really wrestle with the spiritual questions in your life. If you think of depression as a mental and physical resistance to being with the moment, you begin to appreciate how powerful it is to let the resistance be the teacher. This phrase, "letting resistance be the teacher," suggests having the capacity to tune into what is arising in the mind and body and allowing those thoughts and physical sensations to exist, rather than trying desperately to avoid them with perhaps alcohol abuse, the pursuit of a new purchase, or any number of avoidance behaviors that are widely available in our culture. Indeed, it's the direct experience of the body and mind, whether it is the sensation of the warm open heart or the fear in the pit of the belly, which transforms our lives. These direct experiences are transformative because, in the language of Zen, they are moments where the ego has dropped away. We are *just life* at that moment—neither improving life nor rejecting life—just being life.

Now that you have tasted the combo plate, a plate filled with observational skills that develops the muscle of awareness, you will be guided into how these skills can be put into place to help you heal from depression. In the next chapter we will integrate these basics of CBT and mindfulness to give you the greatest possibility to usefully apply them to your daily life.

3

CBT and mindfulness meditation: first steps

You probably don't remember the first steps you took as a toddler or the hard preparation you did as an infant to make you strong enough to begin walking. As with every new skill, it doesn't come at once. New skills take preparation, practice, and motivation. The good news is that both cognitive behavioral therapy and mindfulness meditation have several key skills that can be learned pretty easily. This chapter explains those skills and provides exercises for learning them.

As you go through this and the following chapters, it will be very helpful if you record your thoughts, feelings, and behaviors. At various points we will provide you with exercises to complete. We all know how easy it is to read exercises and think, "that sounds good," but never actually try them. Please try to do the exercises, as you will have a much better chance to learn something by actually working through them, rather than just reading about them. In addition, it's useful to get a simple notebook or scratch pad that you can keep with you so that you can write down thoughts, feelings, and actions that are important throughout the day. One client who drives a great deal keeps a voice-activated recorder with him. When he notices a negative emotion he wants to understand, he records the feeling and any thoughts on his recorder so he can remember it for later.

It is very important to track your experiences on paper, by tape recorder, or some other way so that you can go back and review them. The reason for recording is simple. People who are depressed have problems with memory. They not only have a hard time remembering things in general, but they are more likely to notice and remember things that are depressing. If you rely on your memory, you're most likely shooting yourself in the foot. Writing things down helps you get more accurate and helpful information for improving your mood.

Cognitive Behavioral Therapy

CBT is based first on recognizing how different aspects of yourself and the world around you influence your experience. In a way, the first job of CBT is to become a detective, finding out as much as you can about you. You have a big advantage, because unlike other detectives, you get to see what is happening in your mind and body, including all your thoughts and feelings.

We believe (and research supports) that how you think is going to play a role in how you feel and what you do. Since depression is a mood disorder that involves problems in thinking, feeling, and actions, you need to observe all three. There are several ways to do this, and each has some strength. We will present several. You may want to try a couple, and figure out which ones tell you the most useful information about yourself. Following are some suggestions to help you make the most of your observations.

Make Measurements Meaningful

To know if what you're doing is useful, you need to be able to measure change in your thoughts, actions, and feelings. Therefore, you will find it very helpful to define, in measurable terms, what you are observing. If you say, "I will watch what I do," it will be very hard to know exactly what to pay attention to and when. In this situation you have chosen something too broad and general to actually observe. It's much more helpful to say, "I will count each time I make a critical self-comment," or " I will record my activity each hour on the hour." Because these goals are measurable and defined, they are easier to do and it is easier for you to know whether you have actually done them.

Set Realistic Goals

Setting goals is often difficult because when you try new things, you don't usually have the experience to know whether a goal is reasonable or not. In addition, when you feel depressed, you're less likely to think that *anything* is a realistic goal. One way to set a realistic goal for observation is to choose one thing that is pretty easy to notice. In the mindfulness practice, for example, your breath is often the first object of observation. In treating depression, it is often helpful to notice how depressed you feel (on a scale of 0 to 10, for example) at a certain time of day (such as when you wake up). Once you get pretty good at that, you might move on to more things.

Make Careful Choices

Choose to observe something that you think is closely related to your mood. The reason you learn to observe things in CBT is to learn how those things either increase or decrease your depressed mood. Therefore, you want to observe things that you think might relate to your mood. The things that influence how you feel are your thoughts, activities, and interactions with other people. These could all be important things to observe. Below are some ways to learn to observe yourself, keeping in mind the points above.

CBT Tool Chest: Daily Mood Tracking

At the same time each day, record how depressed you feel on a scale from 10 (not at all) to 1 (worst ever). If you prefer, use another emotion (anxious, angry, etc.). Make a note (one short sentence) about anything you think is affecting your mood. A Daily Mood Scale is provided in the appendix to help.

Daily mood tracking is a relatively easy way to start learning about your mood disorder. Over time, you are likely going to see patterns to your mood. These might include situations where your mood gets better or worse, or days (like your day off or your first work day of the week) where your mood changes. Sometimes these are things you already know, but don't be surprised if you notice new things.

Multiple Ratings

Some people find it hard to rate one mood for the day. If that is true for you, you might want to rate your best and worst mood of the day.

Positive Mood

It is also helpful to rate a positive mood (like feeling happy or content). Many people feel that depressed and happy cannot exist at the same time, but others find that they can feel both. (Have you ever seen a movie with a bitter-sweet ending?) Rating both the positive and negative helps you be more aware of your full range of feelings. Mood tracking gives you good practice at noticing how you feel at a particular time of the day. One limitation of mood tracking is that if doesn't necessarily inform you about what caused the bad mood. Thought tracking, which will be covered in upcoming pages, can be more useful in helping you identify the earliest cause of your mood and the later links between your thoughts and your resulting mood.

There are several possible challenges to mood tracking. First, you might find that it is hard to score your mood on a scale. One way to help figure out what a "0" and a "10" mean for you is to think about a time where you weren't unhappy at all and then a time where you felt the worst ever. Then compare how you feel now to those moods. As you get more examples, you can compare them to get more practice in rating your mood.

Another challenge is if your mood changes a lot during the day. In this case, it can be helpful to rate both a high point and a low point.

Emotion Names

Mood tracking involves just rating your overall depression from 0 to 10. However, it is often helpful to label specific emotions because there are many other feelings besides depression that might be giving you trouble. Unfortunately, sometimes you might not be sure what you feel. If you find it hard to know what your emotions are, you can practice noticing and then putting a name to your feelings.

The emotions on the tables below are just suggestions. You might be able to think of other words that work for you.

Emotions that you might feel when you are depressed

Depression	Anxious	Anger
Sad	Scared	Annoyed
Unhappy	Fearful	Rageful
Hopeless	Nervous	Irritable
Bored	Jumpy	Disgusted
Miserable	Vulnerable	Hateful

Below are some pleasant emotions:

Happy	Excited	Peaceful
Joyful	Energized	Relaxed
Pleased	Pumped Up	Calm
Thrilled	Invigorated	Content
Glad	Intense	Open
Cheerful	Enthusiastic	Mellow

Labeling your feelings helps because you can then learn just how you are affected by different experiences. Let's look at an example. Suppose a friend calls and cancels your lunch date. If we compare two people to whom this happens, both might say they feel "bad." However, if you look closer, you might find there is a difference. If person A feels angry, and person B feels anxious, it tells you that they are reacting to the same event (a canceled lunch) in different ways. What would lead to these different feelings? Probably what person A and person B are telling themselves. Person A is possibly thinking something like, "He shouldn't do that to me," whereas person B might be thinking, "I wonder if I did something wrong?" By noticing the specific emotion you feel, you can then learn to trace back from your feelings to what you are telling yourself, and then you can try and evaluate your thoughts (as you will see in chapter 4).

If you find it hard to label your feelings, you can copy these tables and put them in your notebook. You can also write them on a three-by-five card that you can keep in your pocket. As you get used to observing your emotions it will soon become easier to name them.

Activity Tracking

Since activities often play a big role in how people feel, it is very helpful to learn to track them. Tracking activities can be hard work, but we find it often yields great results.

We ask people to track activities every hour from the time they get up to the time they go to sleep. Doing this gives you a "diary" of your day that helps you see how you spend your time. In addition, we ask you to rate your mood (like above for mood tracking) for each activity. To do this, first write down the activity and then rate your mood following the activity from 0 to 10. This exercise can be easier if you carry a calendar or day planner, and you just add the activity tracking to it. If you don't carry a day planner, it can be very helpful to get one or use a sheet of paper that lists days on top and times down the side. Consider the example below.

What do you learn from activity tracking? It depends on what you're facing. You might be telling yourself, "I'm not doing anything," or, "I never get enough done." Tracking your activities is a nice way to check out whether these thoughts have merit. In addition you can learn what activities or interactions change your mood. You might find that your mood is always worst when you are alone. Alternatively, you might find that your mood is worst when you are with people. Noticing these patterns can help you change your activities so you can feel better.

Scale: 0 = no depression 10 = severe depression		
Time\day	Monday	Tuesday
8:00 A.M.	Woke up 7 Shower 5 Ate breakfast 4	Woke up 6 Shower 4 Breakfast (kids argued) 7
9:00 A.M.	Commute (bad traffic) 7 Got to work late 8	Commute (ok traffic) 3 Work on time 2 Checked messages 2
10:00 A.M.	Meeting 4	Called suppliers 5
11:00 A.M.	Read email 3 Finished report 2	Called suppliers 5

When using a tracking form, the more detail the better. Sometimes people say, "I didn't record X because it seemed so unimportant." Remember, depression often tells you that things are unimportant or don't help when they really do. By recording even normal, everyday things (like taking a shower), you see how they relate to your mood. It is best if you can fill out your form every hour on the hour. If this is not feasible, then try and do it at the end of the day. Each day usually only takes about ten minutes to fill out.

Thought Tracking: Catching the Thought

Many people find that noticing their thinking is the hardest part of cognitive therapy. In part, that is why mindfulness can be such an important addition to cognitive therapy, because it provides very useful skills in observing your thinking.

We have found that it's helpful to start tracking your thoughts in a structured way. To start noticing your thoughts, it is helpful to choose a specific time when you will start. If you know there is a particular time or place where you will likely feel depressed, that is a good opportunity to practice tracking your thoughts. At that time and place, write down three things:

✦ The situation (for instance, where you are, who else is there, what is the activity).

✦ Any feelings you notice (angry, sad, happy, etc.) and how strongly you feel them (from 0 = not at all to 10 = as strong as possible).

✦ Catch the thought: what you are telling yourself or thinking about the situation?

You might find it easy to notice your thoughts, or you might notice lots of thoughts all at once. If the latter is the case, pay particular attention to the thoughts that seem to be related to the feelings you're experiencing. When you move into making change, it will be these thoughts with which you'll work.

On the other hand, you might find it very hard to notice your thoughts. If this is the case, you can try asking yourself the following questions to figure out what you're thinking:

✦ What might I be telling myself that would make me feel what I'm feeling in this situation?

✦ Could I imagine feeling differently in this situation? What might I be telling myself that is preventing me from feeling differently?

✦ Have I responded to similar situations differently? What am I telling myself now that is different from what I told myself then?

One thing that is often hard is figuring out what is a thought and what is a feeling. We tend to use the terms "I think" and "I feel" to mean the same thing. In CBT, it's really important that you notice the difference between what you feel (the emotions and physical sensations you have) and what you think (the things you tell yourself and images that pop into your head). By separating these things, you can figure out how one affects the other.

If you find that you cannot identify a thought or two, then it might make sense to try another situation. In addition, some of the mindfulness exercises may be particularly helpful in increasing your ability to notice your thoughts.

Let's see how Bob does when he tries activity and mood tracking.

Bob has been noticing that he feels sad and blue, both while at work and when he gets home. He decides to start tracking his mood and the situations when it tends to get worse. Since he uses a day planner to write down all the activities of his day, Bob decides to write down, next to each entry in his calendar, a score of 0 (no depression) to 10 (severe depression). After a week, Bob notices four things. First, he is very depressed at his first work meeting each day, but seems to feel better during his later activities. Second, he usually doesn't schedule anything for himself outside of work. He realized that since he didn't have anything planned, he didn't do much after work and ended up feeling particularly bad at night. Third, he noticed that one good day occurred when he got up early and went to the gym before work. Fourth, on the weekend he went with his wife to a lunch with friends. Although he didn't want to go, he went anyway and actually enjoyed it more than anything else that week.

Learning to observe yourself is the groundwork for making change. However, in CBT, we find that observing yourself often improves your mood right away. If that happens for you, great! If not, there is plenty ahead that will help you use your observations to change things.

Start Small

Choose one of the CBT observation techniques and practice it each day. If you want to start simply, use the Daily Mood Scale. If you have thoughts about your activities, either that you are doing too much or too little, use an activity tracking form. If you do not seem to have trouble with your activities, consider trying to catch your thoughts.

Where This is All Going: Experiments

Once you have learned these skills of observation, you will then start moving on to the goal of making changes. One of the most powerful tools in CBT is the ability to create experiments to test out your beliefs and generate new, more healthy and accurate thoughts. In the next four chapters we will be introducing you to the additional CBT tools you'll need to consider using to make your experiments successful. But before we go into details about how to change behavior, we first want to let you know a little about what we mean by an experiment. In science, an experiment is a specific test where you change one thing while holding everything else the same. This allows you to accurately measure the effect of the change. The test is based on a hypothesis, which is just a prediction of how one thing will affect another. For example, you could have the hypothesis that CBT reduces depression. To see if this is true, you could give a group of people CBT training and then measure the change in depression over time to see if it improves. To determine if the depression has improved, you measure it with questionnaires or interviews that are shown to detect depressive symptoms. However, to be an effective experiment, you also have to see what happens to people who do not learn CBT, because everyone might have gotten better anyway.

In this example, there are four critical parts. The first is the hypothesis (CBT reduces depression), the second part is the change (introducing CBT), the third is the comparison condition (the control group), and the fourth is the measurement of the effect of change (using the depression questionnaire). Your hypothesis tells you what you are going to change and what you think will happen. By defining a clear hypothesis, you increase the chance that you will get a clear answer. You then need to test the hypothesis by implementing the change, because this is what you hope will improve things. However, you also need the comparison, because without it you don't know whether any improvement is due to your activity or due to something else. And you need to measure your change in a meaningful way, or else you can't be sure that your activity really is improving things.

Finally, there is one other principle. You can't only try things one time and consider that a valid experiment. For any one attempt, many other things might influence your outcome. To truly test whether an activity is helpful or a belief is true or false, you need to give it a few tries to determine whether there is any benefit.

You can apply this to your own life. First, you can treat your thoughts and beliefs as hypotheses to be tested. Then, come up with a prediction based on the hypothesis, and figure out an experiment that will test the prediction and a way to measure the outcome. Once you do the experiment, you can determine whether your thought (hypothesis) was true, or whether you need a new hypothesis. By actually testing it out, you are likely to have more faith in the new thought than if someone just tells you a different way to think. We encourage you to think of all the activities and exercises in this book as potential experiments. Use them as chances to test out your beliefs and to learn new things about yourself.

Mindfulness Meditation Practice: The Basics

We have talked about how to use your skills of observation by implementing the tools of CBT and the importance of conducting experiments. Shifting gears, we now want to introduce you to some considerations about how to start a mindfulness meditation practice. While observation is key to both CBT and mindfulness meditation, the reasons for observing can be quite different in each discipline. Surely, you want to make your observations accurate and precise using the CBT model to help you change. Whereas, in mindfulness meditation, you also want to make your observations precise to clearly see who you are, so you can be true to yourself without necessarily trying to change. Again, remember that in mindfulness meditation you are observing yourself nonjudgmentally. From the vantage point of a nonjudgmental lens of observation, mindfulness meditation may give you access to your open heart to observe the wide range of your being. This sounds nice, and it is nice, but like all disciplines there is nitty-gritty to a practice, which we will now explore.

Your Position

To get started with a meditation practice you need to start simply and practically. Find a place where you can sit undisturbed for a short period of time. You can start meditating anywhere from five minutes to thirty minutes a day. As we mentioned earlier, when developing a new behavior you want to make your goal modest so you can be successful. Don't make your goal for the length of time or quality of awareness so grand that you cannot be successful in this initial phase of learning to meditate. It's more advantageous to practice five minutes every day than to practice 30 minutes once a week.

It can be helpful to create an atmosphere that is conducive to meditation. You may want to place symbols in the area that help you create a space for meditation, perhaps a flower, an image that has meaning for you, or a candle.

You can start by sitting upright in a chair, or if you are able to and wish to you can sit cross-legged on a meditation cushion on the floor. What is important, however you sit, is that your back is straight and your chest is open so that you can breath fully and easily. If sitting in a chair, place your feet on the ground, and if sitting on a cushion, try to have your knees rest on the floor. If your knees are unable to rest on the floor, you probably need to sit a bit higher, and perhaps you need to place another pillow under your knees so they are supported.

Once you have settled into a basic position, let your upper body gently rock back and forth a few minutes, slowly finding the point where you are centered over your lower body. Let your belly relax. Allow your chest to open by slightly pulling the shoulder blades down the back of your body. Allow your head to rise gently upward from the spine, as though a helium balloon was attached to the crown of the head, providing a subtle upward lift. Try to avoid bending your neck forward and allowing your chest to collapse because this position makes it more difficult to maintain a clear awareness or breathe fully and naturally. Let your body be relaxed and firm, but not rigid. You can mentally scan through your body and notice if there are any sensations of tension or holding, and let those areas relax as best you can. You can either let your eyes close or keep them open with a soft focus, about four feet in front of where you are sitting.

Your Breath

Once you have found a posture that you can easily maintain for the length of time you want to sit, bring your attention to your breath. Let the breath be natural and not forced. Developing the capacity to concentrate and focus is an important early part of learning to meditate. The breath is most frequently the suggested focal point for placing your attention because it is a bodily function that is constantly occurring in this moment. Again, the training of the mind and body to rest in this moment is a primary goal for a mindfulness meditation practice, which is why this practice is rooted in a physical sensation that can always guide you back to the present moment. You will soon see that your body is your home in practice, and that through mindfulness you will be learning to rest in this home.

There are many ways to bring your attention to your breath. There are no hard and fast rules about the best ways to develop awareness of the breath. Some initial suggestions for placing your attention on the breath include the following:

✦ Pay attention to the movement of the air in and out of your nostrils, feeling the sensation of the cool air coming in and the warm air flowing out.

✦ Count the breaths coming in and flowing out in a cycle from one to ten, and then repeat this cycle for the period of time you are meditating. This can be done several ways. You can breath in on one and breath out on two, or you can count one for the full cycle of your breath. It is very common to not get to "two" before the mind has wandered off, so don't be hard on yourself should you notice this happening. Simply notice the wandering mind, and go back to your counting, either starting your counting back where you left off, or returning to one.

✦ Notice the full cycle of the breath and all the sensations associated with the movement of your breath. Attention can be given to the breath in great detail. Explore where in your body you first feel the first impulse to breathe in. Notice how the breath moves into your body. Notice where you feel your breath and where you don't feel your breath. Do you feel your breath in the front part of your chest and belly, or do you also notice the breath move into the side ribs and the back of your body? What happens to your shoulders as you breathe in and out? Does your mind tend to wander as you inhale? As you exhale? What happens to your body as you breathe more deeply?

✦ For a cycle of three breaths notice sensations associated with three different places in your body. For example, on the first breath notice sensations in your face and any sensations of the air against your face. On the second breath, move your attention to any sensations in your chest area. For the third breath, place your attention on sensations in the lower half of your body. As you shift your attention to these different parts, you can use both the sensations arising from your body, and the sensations from where your body has contact with the furniture or the ground to anchor your attention.

Do one of the above suggestions at a time. People often find that it's difficult to concentrate when the mind is very active. If the mind is active or even agitated it can be helpful to give the mind a number of things to be aware of, such as counting breaths both in and out. Certainly do not be limited to these suggestions in the exploration of your breath. The goal is for you to become intimate with the flow of your breath in your body. The movement of the breath is a key tool for mindfulness practice, as well as for your general health.

In the initial phases of sitting (and even after many years) it's astonishing to notice how difficult it is to stay with the breath, because the mind is inclined to wander off into thinking. (In future chapters we will discuss in greater detail how to work with the thoughts that arise.) But for now, let's discuss how you deal with the drifting mind.

The Drifting Mind

When the mind drifts off into thinking, simply notice that you are no longer aware of the breath and try to bring your attention back to your breath. This is easier said then done. Why? Because we have critical minds that are usually judging the quality of our awareness and thinking about the thoughts that are running through our minds.

For example, let's say you are meditating and you notice the sound of traffic outside your room. The sound of traffic leads you to think about your car, and that your car needs to be serviced. Then you start thinking about where you can get your car serviced and whether or not you can afford that expense at this moment. Then suddenly you remember the breath and realize that you are no longer aware of your breathing, which leads you to have a judgmental thought like, "I can't keep focused on my breath." This is a moment in a meditation practice where people often feel like a failure. In actuality it is moment of triumph, because it's a moment where the light of awareness can help you clearly perceive what is happening in this moment. It is an opportune moment to recognize that you are now judging yourself. Once you recognize that you're having judgmental thoughts you can notice how these thoughts affect you. For example, you may further notice that this judgment actually increases your anxiety and agitation, or you may notice that you now feel discouraged and like a failure. At this moment you become aware of your thoughts, feel the sensations in your body, and generally notice where the mind has wandered. After you take a moment to become aware of what is occurring in your mind and body, then simply return your attention to the breath.

As meditation practice develops there are a variety of other ways to cope with and ultimately learn from the wandering mind. But in the initial phases it's most helpful to notice that the mind has wandered and to perceive these wanderings as events or patterns, and then to let the focus return back to the breath. How to note the wandering mind will be further discussed in chapter 4.

A common misconception for the novice meditator is to think that if their mind has wandered then he or she has failed. Particularly if the new meditator also happens to be depressed, then the likelihood of having negative thoughts about the quality of the meditation will likely be high. We cannot state enough that the mind wanders even after years of extensive practice. A quality that is helpful to bring to the wandering mind is kindness. As much as possible, try to watch the wanderings with kindness and compassion.

The Body Scan

There are numerous pathways for entering the world of mindfulness meditation. Many people have been introduced to mindfulness by learning how to do a body scan. The body scan was first introduced to America when the "Healing and the Mind Series," produced by Bill Moyers in the early 90s, followed the progress of a stress reduction class taught by Jon Kabat-Zinn. Kabat-Zinn's book, *Full Catastrophe Living* (1990), describes in great detail the Mindfulness-Based Stress Reduction Program, which is the model for programs taught around the world, including the one at the VA Medical Center in San Diego. This approach to stress reduction teaches nonjudgmental awareness through three primary vehicles: the body scan, sitting meditation, and yoga.

A body scan is a seemingly simple activity. Generally, you lie down and move your mental awareness through your body, starting on one end and slowly moving your attention to the other end. As you move your attention through the body you try to be aware of any sensations that might be present in that particular spot of the body. You don't try to create sensations or think about what a sensation means, why you may not feel anything in that part of the body, or even try to make yourself relax. Rather, you use your attention to focus on what sensations are present and then move on.

There can be a paradoxical quality to the body scan. As described above, you are not trying to force relaxation. However, as you learn to become more sensitive to sensations in your body and particularly to the flow of your breath, relaxation is often increased. This relaxation can be spread through your body by using your "mind's eye" to move your breath into different places in your body as you move your attention through your physical self.

The body scan helps you become more sensitive to different sensations in your body. It also helps you learn to hang out with a variety of sensations, whether they are pleasant or unpleasant. This willingness to approach unpleasant sensations is a powerful way to start deconditioning our persistent avoidance of pain, be it physical or mental pain. When you get interested in the sensation, just the pure quality of the tingling, the tightness, or where the sensation starts and where it ends, you start to decrease the fear often associated with painful sensations. This decrease in fear is very helpful for dealing with painful physical or emotional situations. When fear is at your side but not crouching over you in a menacing manner, your body can unwind enough to let the unpleasantness be there, but not be overwhelming. You can breathe into the painful places, stay with the unpleasant sensations, and then breathe out, noting any change in intensity of the sensation. In this way, painful sensations are "touched" through the breath, experienced, and allowed to exist in the field of awareness.

You might wonder why there is all this emphasis on the body. You might even question what good it does for you, especially if you are depressed. If you're depressed, you are likely to have restricted awareness of sensations in your body. Possibly you could be caught up in negative thinking and quite unaware of what is going on below your head. The body scan is a helpful means for you to begin to feel connected to your body. Not only does the body scan enhance awareness of your body; it cultivates flexible and focused attention by training you to shift your attention throughout your body. In a certain way, it is like doing yoga with your mind and body without moving, because like yoga, you have to spread your awareness through your body. You will see in later chapters that the flexibility of attention developed by the body scan will be a helpful quality of the mind to have cultivated when working towards acceptance of difficult life circumstances.

The body scan is not an athletic achievement. When you do it, you're not trying to purify the body with a magical breath or develop astonishing powers of awareness. While you will likely feel more relaxed and aware because of the attention you have given your body, the real intention is to wake up to your body, not improve it. You can notice any strivings you have in connection to doing the body scan and just let those take a back seat while doing the body scan. Like all mindfulness practices, you do the body scan to be fully present in the moment, awakening to how your body is feeling right now.

Having a voice guide you through the body scan is very helpful. We suggest you either produce your own tape by recording your voice doing the body scan out loud or purchase a tape or CD through the Center for Mindfulness Web site mentioned in the appendix. It is more difficult to do the body scan unguided, so a recording is a big help.

To give you a sense of the body scan we have given you some general instructions on how to do it. These instructions are abbreviated for *Peaceful Mind* due to space considerations. People can take as long as forty-five minutes to do a body scan, or they can learn to quickly scan through the body in a matter of moments. The guidance given here is generally geared to allow you to do the scan in about a half hour. (When you move through each limb separately, the process becomes longer, and it is obviously shorter when you move your attention through both limbs simultaneously. We suggest when starting out that you pay attention to each limb separately.)

A common problem people encounter when doing the body scan is that they fall asleep. When teaching the body scan, it's common to have people snoring away during the class! If you find that you're falling asleep when you try the scan, there are a few suggestions to consider. Try keeping your eyes open. Don't scan just before bed, unless your intention is to use it to make you relaxed enough to fall asleep. If you are snoozing through the body scan one problem could be that you are doing it on your bed and there is too much of an association between sleep and your bed. Consider doing it on the floor, a couch, or a mat.

Instructions for the Body Scan

✦ As you prepare to do the body scan please remember that this is a time you can use to be with yourself, perhaps in a new and meaningful way. It's important not to try too hard to relax, as this will probably create tension. Be aware of each moment, letting go of any tendency to want things to be different. Allow yourself to be sensitive to any sensations you feel as you move your attention through your body.

✦ It is very normal to feel connected to some parts of your body and quite disconnected from others. Don't worry about this. There will be instructions about breathing into certain body parts. If these instructions feel odd to you or you're worrying about not doing them right, please try to just notice those thoughts and let your worries go.

✦ Your mind will inevitably wander during the body scan. When this happens, just gently note that your mind has wandered off and bring your attention back to the body scan.

✦ Lie down on your back on a bed, mat, or couch. Notice how your body meets the surface upon which you are lying. Feel your body as a whole, from your head to your toes and from the back of your body to the front of your body.

✦ You can close your eyes or you can keep them open. Do whatever helps you to maintain awareness.

✦ Bring your attention to your breath, feeling the rhythmic movement of the breath as it flows in and out of your body. Feel your breath move in and out of your chest and abdomen. Do this for a few minutes.

✦ As you move your attention to different parts of your body, use your breath as a physical link to guide the movement of your attention to the place in the body where you are placing your mental awareness.

✦ Now bring your focus down you left leg to your left foot. Bring your attention to your left toes, first your big toe and then moving through all the toes of you left foot. Notice any sensations of warmth, tingling, coolness, or perhaps the lack of sensation in your toes. Now move your attention into the ball of the foot, the arch of the foot, and the heel of the foot. Allow your attention to expand to the top of foot and then move your focus into the ankle. Breathe with any sensations present in the left foot.

✦ When you are ready, let your attention shift from the left foot and move your awareness up your left leg, keeping the same kind of detailed awareness of sensations as you shift your attention up to the calf, the knee, the thigh, and up into your hips.

✦ In the same detailed manner, move your attention down to your right toes and back up your right leg with the same degree of focus and care that you gave your left foot and leg.

✦ Now move your attention into your hips. Allow your awareness to move up into your pelvic region. Notice any sensations in your genital area. With a sense of gentle curiosity, move your attention up through your spine and then sideways, out the backside of your body. Shifting your focus to the front of your body, feel into your chest. Feel your heart in your body, your lungs breathing. Notice the sensations throughout your chest.

✦ Now bring your mind to your upper arms . . . your elbows . . . forearms . . . wrists . . . and the palms of your hands. Feel into each of your fingers. Let your breath move down into and out of your fingers.

✦ Now allow your attention to move up into your neck. Feel sensations in the front of your throat and in the back of your neck.

✦ Now focus your attention to the sensations in your head. Notice where you have sensations and where you don't have sensations. Bring your attention to your scalp. Now move your awareness to your ears, noticing the sensations of hearing. Allow your attention to shift to your forehead, breathing into your face, noticing how the breath affects sensations in your face. Guide your awareness to your eyes . . . your nose . . . feeling the breath move in and out of your nostrils.

✦ Now let your focus gently relax and expand to feel your entire body at once. Let go of any control of the breath, the breath moving freely in and out of the body, being your body as it is in this moment.

From *Full Catastrophe Living* by Jon Kabat-Zinn, copyright © 1990 by Jon Kabat-Zinn. Used by permission of Dell Publishing, a division of Random House, Inc.

We are now going to shift from experiencing the physical structure of your body through doing the body scan to looking at the psychological structure of yourself through the core belief framework. As you read through the next chapter, consider how you physically feel the psychological components in your body. Make photocopies of this form and use it to track your mood.

4

core belief framework

Understanding the framework and pervasive influence of your core beliefs is a major step toward freeing yourself from the web of depression. As we explained earlier, your core beliefs are deeply believed self-concepts that greatly influences both how you perceive yourself and what you tend to pay attention to in your internal thoughts and in your interactions with others.

Aaron Beck, his daughter Judith Beck, and others have written extensively about core beliefs. Charlotte Joko Beck (no relationship), Ezra Bayda, and Elizabeth Hamilton have used a similar model of core beliefs in their descriptions of Zen practice. We will look at a model that has four levels: core beliefs, assumptions, strategies, and automatic thoughts. We will see how these four levels are functioning by looking at a case example. After the core belief framework has been presented, we will look at how the tools of CBT and mindfulness meditation can be applied to coping with depression.

Core Beliefs

At the deepest level, most hidden from your view, are your core beliefs. They are like hidden groundwater that runs deep beneath the earth, invisibly feeding all of your assumptions, strategies, and automatic thoughts. Although core beliefs are not readily seen, they are nonetheless extremely powerful. Everybody has one or more core beliefs. Core beliefs are developed at a young age, usually in a child's effort to organize their world based upon how the people around them are responding. Young children all strive to be attached to their parents and will learn about themselves and the world around them depending on how their attempts to be attached are treated. Early acceptance can lead to core beliefs about being valued, while rejection could lead to beliefs such as, "The world is cruel," or, "I am unlovable." Core beliefs can be born from difficult conditions of early life like poverty, neglect, or exposure to trauma. The inevitable hardships and losses in life lead every young child to make conclusions about how to engage with others to get what they think they want. All people develop core beliefs, which guide you in your efforts to be liked, loved, accepted, respected, and feel in control. These beliefs are so integral to the fibers of your being that you perceive them as the absolute truth.

Just as everybody who is living has a heart, everybody who is living has some sort of core belief. Typically when people first become aware of their core beliefs, they assume there is something wrong with them for having them. We encourage you to use your heart of compassion as you notice your core beliefs and any critical thoughts you might have about them. The same nonjudgmental stance is very helpful as you learn to observe all the four levels of your core belief system.

In *Cognitive Therapy: Basics and Beyond* (1995) Judith Beck has conceptualized core beliefs associated with depression as being divided into two broad areas: helplessness core beliefs and unlovable core beliefs. When you are depressed the defenses that normally protect you from feeling the vulnerability of your core beliefs are weakened, and therefore you are more likely to believe them without question. Consider the following examples of core beliefs as described by Judith Beck.

Helpless Core Beliefs

I am helpless.	I am inadequate.
I am powerless.	I am ineffective.
I am out of control.	I am incompetent.
I am weak.	I am a failure.
I am vulnerable.	I am disrespectful.

I am needy.

I am defective (for instance,
I have some damage or flaw).

I am trapped.

I am not good enough
(in terms of achievement).

Unlovable Core Beliefs

I am unlovable.

I am unworthy.

I am unlikable.

I am different.

I am undesirable.

I am defective (so others
will not love me).

I am unattractive.

I am not good enough
(to be loved by others).

I am unwanted.

I am bound to be rejected.

I am uncared for.

I am bound to be abandoned.

I am bad.

I am bound to be alone.

Let's look at how Emily developed her core beliefs. Emily entered therapy at the age of thirty-five. She had been practicing mindfulness meditation for the past year. She was distressed by the number of worries she had regarding how she was perceived by her peers. A sensitive person, she works as a paralegal in a law firm, doing her best to meet the many demands of a fast-paced office. Emily has the core belief that she is not wanted. Emily was born into a large family; she is the fourth child of five children. Her mother started back to work when Emily was three years old. Emily felt angry when she was forced to go to nursery school whereas her older brothers and sisters had been able to stay home with their mother. After starting a career, her mother became busy and anxious about work and thus was preoccupied and not able to give much attention to Emily or her siblings. Emily concluded that she was not wanted, and that this was the reason why her mom went back to work.

What can be perplexing about core beliefs is that there can be evidence that disproves the belief. For example, in Emily's situation, an outside observer could see evidence that she was loved and an important member of the family. However, Emily's core belief was developed at a young age and because there was sufficient evidence to support her beliefs of being unwanted she could not deeply accept the other truth, that she was loved. When basic truths exist for children, life experience is then sorted through those different perspectives, and like the outer shaft of the wheat, one truth is easily cast to the wind. Now we will look at how core beliefs support the remaining framework.

Assumptions

Assumptions are the rules you make for how you conduct yourself based upon your core beliefs. Assumptions influence your characteristic thinking and reactions to situations. Whereas core beliefs may not be at a conscious level, assumptions typically are at a conscious level of awareness. How you perceive others and what you believe they think of you is driven by your assumptions. Assumptions are part of your everyday thinking, and therefore they can be easier than core beliefs to recognize, challenge, and shift. Because they are more on the surface of your awareness, assumptions can hint at your underlying core beliefs and help you predict likely scenarios in your thinking and behaviors.

If core beliefs are represented by the vast groundwater, assumptions are the springs of water flowing up from the groundwater of the core beliefs to the surface of your awareness. These springs bubble up to the earth, sometimes in dark and murky places, but other times they are wide out in the open, visible to everyone.

Emily held the assumptions that the world was largely unsafe and that it was dangerous to trust people. These assumptions flowed from her core belief that she was not wanted, because the core belief predisposed her to be wary of her environment and her relationships with others. As an adolescent and young adult, Emily often felt left out, perceived that people didn't like her, and had difficulties making close friends. At the age of thirty-five she had been married and divorced, and after a recent break-up with a boyfriend, she became so depressed that she started therapy. She had difficulty sharing much with her therapist because she made the assumption that her therapist was only interested in seeing her because she had insurance to pay for twenty sessions. She didn't trust the therapist and had difficulty understanding why she felt so anxious at work. She was largely unaware that she had been operating at work under the assumption that people would reject her.

Whereas Emily couldn't immediately identify her core belief that she felt unwanted, she came to acknowledge that she felt distrustful of others and was likely to assume that others would reject her. Now, as we move on to discuss strategies, you will see that there is a variety of strategies that people can have based upon their core beliefs and assumptions.

Strategies

Strategies are defensive styles or chronic behaviors that protect the individual from feeling the pain of a core belief. Strategies are your basic, most consistent responses to everyday events. They are logical actions given your core beliefs and assumptions. Strategies tend to be embedded patterns with a pervasive influence, and when not clearly recognized as strategies, they are very difficult to change. When people say such things as, "She is reliable," "He is only worried about himself," "He can be counted on to do the job," "She is a control freak," they are making comments about your behavior that might reflect a defending strategy.

Again, just like with core beliefs, strategies are not "bad," or anything to be embarrassed about. In fact, strategies generally are reasonable responses to your perception that your core beliefs and assumptions are true. When learning about your strategies, view them with mindfulness, seeing them as behaviors not to be judged as good or bad. It is very helpful to use a quality of warmth towards yourself as you uncover your strategies.

Why is it helpful to recognize the strategies operating in your life? If you're depressed, you may be using strategies that previously worked for you, but in the current moment actually make your depression worse. For example, you may have the strategy to avoid conflicts, and now that you are depressed you have completely withdrawn from not only conflicts, but from people and activities in general. This strategy to avoid any possible conflict has spread to all activities and has intensified your depression. If you have ever found yourself saying, "Why the heck did I do that? That was stupid," you were likely using an old, well-practiced strategy without realizing that it wasn't the right choice in the situation. When working for relief from depression, understanding your strategies will help you consider behavioral targets. When you focus in on these unhelpful behaviors and begin to change them, your depression will ease.

Strategies can be perceived as the current of the river, fed from the spring of assumptions and the subterranean groundwater of core beliefs. Strategies, like the river, are on the surface, visible to all who gaze upon them. One does not directly recognize the influence of either the vast groundwater (the core belief) or the bubbling spring (the assumptions), but these pressures are nonetheless exerting their influence upon the current of the river. The river's current may change with the seasons, the amount of rainfall, and any shifts to the terrain either upstream or downstream. The current of the river is not thinking about how it's going to flow; it is flowing in the style that it knows best, usually moving down the path of least resistance. Like the river, you usually don't think about your strategy. The strategy is just the way you do things, and to do otherwise would feel like being someone you don't know.

Emily had defended against her core belief of being unwanted and her assumption that people will reject her by using the strategy of being overly nice, pleasant, and hardworking. This primary strategy stemmed from the assumption, "If I keep people happy they won't reject me." She tried hard to please others and was skilled in reading the nuances of communication in others so she could behave in a fashion that would get their approval. She was particularly sensitive to feeling rejected and often misinterpreted her colleagues questions as criticism. When she felt criticized she rarely became angry and defensive (another strategy possibility); rather she more often felt victimized and thought life was unfair. In therapy she tended to complain to her therapist about how she was treated unfairly by both her ex-boyfriend and her colleagues at work. In her mindfulness meditation practice, she would find that her mind would frequently wander to the injustices of her life. Underneath her surface pleasantness she was vaguely aware of her deeper pessimism regarding her relationships and her future.

A crucial component for understanding a core belief system is recognizing that the same core belief can drive different strategies and that one person may have different strategies operating at different times in their life. Furthermore, depending upon the situation, someone may have a different strategy in use at different times in a day. However, people typically have a primary strategy that is in a sense the first line of defense, and when that fails they will draw upon alternative strategies. However, if you trace the motivating drive behind the strategy, you will quickly encounter the shadow of the core belief. (This is further illustrated in the Core Belief Framework Tables presented later in this chapter.) Strategies can have different relationships to the core belief. They may work to maintain a core belief, oppose a core belief, or avoid a core belief. In Emily's situation, her strategy was to oppose her core belief of believing she was unwanted by working hard to keep people happy so they wouldn't reject her. Alternatively, she could have developed the strategy of supporting her core belief by developing the strategy of being overly critical and harsh toward others, thus acting in a way that would increase the likelihood that others would reject her, thus affirming her belief. Another option would be for her to choose a lifestyle where there was minimal interaction with others, thus attempting to avoid the tension of experiencing her core belief.

Automatic Thoughts

Automatic thoughts are like the fish in the river, darting through your consciousness all the time. Like the fish, automatic thoughts are sometimes on the surface, readily seen, and at other times they are swimming far below where you cannot see them and they avoid being caught. Schools of fish are sometimes present, as thoughts sometimes seem massive and overwhelming. Fish can swim in different directions, sometimes swimming with the current and other times swimming steadfastly against the current. Like the fish darting in the river, automatic thoughts dart across your mind in response to all the large and small issues of your life, sometimes fighting your basic strategies and sometimes just moving with the current of your strategy. Because automatic thoughts are influenced by your strategies, assumptions, and core beliefs, they tend to have repetitive patterns. However, it's not always easy to catch them, as they come and go quickly. Sometimes automatic thoughts can be difficult to recognize because they hit when you're caught up in an emotional state and you may have a hard time perceiving these underlying thoughts. Catching dysfunctional automatic thoughts is a great opportunity for change when you're doing CBT.

Let's take a look at how automatic thoughts affect Emily at work. Her supervising lawyer told Emily that she was not being placed on a new important case because her expertise was needed on a case that was smaller and less prestigious. Emily had the automatic thought, "She doesn't really like me, which is why she isn't putting me on the case." Then later that day on her drive home, she wasn't able to get that notion out of her mind. It even started branching out into other disturbing thoughts like, "Maybe she isn't assigning me to that new case because she is really planning on letting me go. I bet I'm going to be fired." With all of these negative thoughts crowding in, Emily had a great deal of difficulty remembering that her supervisor had actually told her that her expertise was valuable, which was why she was assigned a different case.

Putting Them Together

To give you another way to understand how these factors work together, consider this flow chart that illustrates the dynamic flow of the core belief framework. Here's how Emily's framework looks:

Emily's Framework

Automatic Thoughts (Fish in the river)

She doesn't really like me.

↓

Strategies (Current of the river)

If I keep people happy they won't reject me.

↓

Assumptions (Spring of water)

The world is unsafe, and it is difficult to trust people.

↓

Core Beliefs (Groundwater)

I am unwanted.

Understanding the framework of your core belief system is invaluable when you're trying to work through a depressive episode or even a blue mood. When you have a clear understanding of the framework that guides much of your thinking and behavior, you have far more opportunities to observe the impact of all this conditioning on your everyday life. This clear perception gives you the opportunity to use skills from both CBT and mindfulness meditations to observe, challenge, adapt, and tolerate your core belief framework.

There are many variations of core beliefs, as we saw in the list of core beliefs. The following Core Belief Frameworks provide you some examples of how core beliefs, assumptions, strategies, and automatic thoughts might play out in different people. These examples are intended to provide an overview of the interplay of the dynamics driven by the core belief, but are not intended to be an exhaustive list. We encourage you to map out your own core belief framework using the following model. This work draws on the schema model of Jeffrey Young (1990).

Framework for the Core Belief, "I'm inadequate."

Strategies	Assumptions	Automatic Thoughts
MAINTAINING STRATEGY Never tries hard. Procrastinates. Sets up self for failure.	Others are better. I'll never succeed.	"I failed again." "I can't do that." "She can do it better then I can; I won't try."
OPPOSING STRATEGY Works hard. Is pleasant. Uses humor to win people.	I'll have to work harder then everybody else.	"I was just lucky when I succeeded."
AVOIDING STRATEGY Takes unchallenging jobs. Settles for relationships that are not deeply satisfying. Doesn't ask for much.	It doesn't matter if I succeed or fail. Someone else will figure it out.	"I don't really care." "I'm not sure what to do." "I'll just wait and see what happens."

Framework for the Core Belief, "I'm Unworthy."

Strategies	Assumptions	Automatic Thoughts
MAINTAINING STRATEGY Chooses partners who are rejecting. Leaves relationships and friendships quickly.	No one can really love me. I'm not good enough.	"I'm doomed to be alone." "It's not fair." "I'll fail."
OPPOSING STRATEGY Falls in love easily and works hard to stay in difficult relationships. Works long and hard and performs well in employment.	I am basically flawed, so I have to try very hard to be loved or get to love someone.	"I don't want to be alone." "I'll prove to them that I'm really good." "I'm doing something wrong."
AVOIDING STRATEGY Avoids relationships. Works alone.	I'm not a people person.	"I've been alone for so long, I'm not going to try to get along with people." "I prefer being by myself."

Framework for the Core Belief, "I'm vulnerable."

Strategies	Assumptions	Automatic Thoughts
MAINTAINING STRATEGY Solicits help from others. Makes decisions by getting other people's opinions. Avoids taking risks or doing challenging activities.	I need others. I can't do it by myself.	"Who can help me?" "This is too hard."
OPPOSING STRATEGY Is self-reliant and defensive. Doesn't ask for help, even when appropriate.	I feel like I need help, but asking for help is bad. Being weak is too risky.	"Look what I did all by myself." "They are so incompetent." "What a jerk he is; he can't do anything."
AVOIDING STRATEGY Being alone is familiar and secure. Develops skills of being a loner. Works alone.	I avoid others. Feeling vulnerable is bad. Relationships will not go well. I'm more efficient and productive working and living alone.	"They wouldn't like or understand me anyway." "I like being by myself."

Diving In: Identifying your Core Belief Framework

Cognitive therapy and mindfulness both provide excellent means for identifying your core belief framework. You begin recognizing your core belief framework by noticing the darting automatic thoughts, and over time you can dive deeper into yourself and more fully understand the groundwater from which this structure was born. Through meditation you can deeply know the groundwater. In this section we will describe how you can use the tools of CBT and mindfulness to help you understand your core belief framework.

To return to our earlier metaphor, you are standing on the bank of the river watching the fish glide under the surface of the river, learning to recognize the automatic thoughts that come and go. You don't have to be doing either CBT or any mindfulness activities to have automatic thoughts; these thoughts are present all the time. They show up in your everyday life, when you are washing the dishes, driving to work, and talking with a neighbor. Doing either CBT or mindfulness meditation helps you to observe and recognize how these automatic thoughts unconsciously run your life. Pretty soon you can watch your mind and say, "Hey, there's a thought," as easily as watching the river and saying, "Hey, there's a fish."

CBT cultivates awareness of your automatic thoughts by reviewing thought records and charting the events in your daily life to learn how thoughts influence your mood. Mindfulness meditation teaches you to persistently note and label your thoughts. By becoming aware of these thoughts you will begin to recognize that there are patterns and themes.

Labeling and Noting

When you meditate or try to be mindful in your daily life you will probably notice there are many thoughts that interrupt your attention. *Thought labeling* is noticing the thoughts that interrupt you from being present in this moment, and is done somewhat differently according to the teacher and tradition. Charlotte Joko Beck and her successors (Ezra Bayda and Elizabeth Hamilton) in general will instruct students to label simply by repeating back the thought that you have, adding the word "thinking" to the beginning of the thought. For example, if you are having the thought, "I cannot do this," you label the thought by saying to yourself, "Thinking I cannot do this." To further undercut your belief in the thought, you can practice labeling by saying, "Having a believed thought that I cannot do this." When you add the term "believed thought," it is a way of highlighting in your mind that this is not only a thought, but that you're choosing to believe that this thought is real. When you let your mind question the validity or accuracy of the thoughts you can then begin to taste the disillusioned world of thoughts and start to turn your attention to the physical reality in which you live. But you cannot begin to rest in a wider field of awareness until you know the thoughts that drive your behavior.

Learning how to watch the mind that is full of thoughts can be done in any number of ways, and it can be useful to experiment with what works well for you. Buddhist teachers such as Jack Kornfield and Sylvia Boorstein describe "noting" thoughts as a way to watch the mind. When you note thoughts you name conditions of the mind, using your attention to note and name what is happening in the present moment. For example, you use mindfulness to note thinking, planning, remembering, worrying, or even happy states such as tranquility or pleasure. The noting is not at the forefront of your attention; it is the backdrop against which observation of each moment occurs. Like labeling, you simply say quietly to yourself that which you are observing, such as "desire . . . desire . . . desire," and then you may recognize that the condition of the mind and body has shifted slightly and now you realize that "worrying . . . worrying . . . worrying," is the accurate word to use to note the mind.

Labeling thoughts and noting the condition of the mind trains you first to recognize where your attention is placed. If you are having a distressing thought, and you realize you're having the thought, you have the opportunity to consider whether it is accurate or real. Secondly, thought labeling helps you recognize the power and pattern of your thinking and the influence it has on your present state of being. While it sounds like a tedious task, these practices of labeling and noting the mind awaken the witness or observer in you and over time weakens the power your thoughts have over you. Thought labeling is done with the same nonjudgmental mind that you use with all mindfulness practice. This is easier said than done, as you will probably notice that there is an array of feelings associated with what you are noting or labeling. You may be saying to yourself, "Hey, I'm getting pretty good at this!" or conversely, "Damn it! There I go judging again." As you note and label your thoughts also be aware of the emotional tone of your observing mind and bring the same nonjudgmental awareness to this whole process. With patience and persistence, these approaches to observing your mind and body will help you understand your core belief framework and develop a gentler attitude toward yourself.

A word of caution: Neither thought labeling nor noting the mind is trying to entice you to think about your thoughts; to the contrary, they are approaches to help you observe the mind and help make thoughts less gripping. However, it is very tempting to start thinking about the thought you have just labeled or even about how to label the thought or note your mental state. Should this occur, just label "thinking about the thought" or note "deciding mind" or "thinking mind." When you're doing a mindfulness practice it is completely normal to find that you have thoughts every few seconds. Even after years of practice it's common to find that you get lost in thoughts or a story line for minutes at a time. You may find that you have thoughts much more frequently and persistently than you ever imagined. Don't be discouraged! Your thought labeling practice is working. Automatic thoughts are frequent and persistent by their very nature. Catching them requires patience and practice. Coming to understand that there is nothing wrong with having thoughts every few seconds is one of the fruits of mindfulness meditation.

Let us consider how Emily learned about her core belief structure using CBT and mindfulness. Emily's first goal was to become aware of the automatic thoughts that influenced her daily mood. She did this in two ways. First she started to keep a simple record of her daily events, moods, and automatic thoughts, and when she practiced mindfulness meditation, she carefully labeled the frequently repeated thoughts. Her daily events, moods, and automatic thoughts were tracked simply in this model, adapted from *Mind over Mood: A Cognitive Therapy Treatment Manual for Clients,* by Dennis Greenberger, Ph.D. and Christine Padesky, Ph.D. (1995).

Emily's Automatic Thoughts		
Events	Moods	Automatic Thoughts
Who? What? When? Where?	What was your mood in relation to the event? Rate your emotion from, 0 to 10, 0 = best mood 10 = worst mood	Record the most immediate thought that went through your mind when you first noticed your mood. Make an asterisk by the strongest thought.
1. My boss told me that I would not be assigned to new case.	Sad, 7	"I bet I'm going to be fired."
2. A colleague invited me to go out for dinner.	Anxious, 5	"I can't imagine that he really wants to go out with me."
3. My mother phoned me up to ask why I hadn't phoned her in two weeks.	Guilty, 8 Angry, 9	"She is only really interested in herself."***

Sometimes it becomes clear from a review of the automatic thoughts that there is a recurrent theme. For example, in the above example it can be deduced that Emily certainly does not feel confident that people want to be with her. She typically assumes that relationships are not going to go well and that even her mother is not genuinely interested in her. We know from the earlier analysis of Emily that she feels unwanted, but Emily is probably not conscious of it. To help her become aware of this core belief, or the groundwater of her being, cognitive therapists have devised a technique that is commonly known as the "downward arrow technique."

The Downward Arrow

The downward arrow technique is a questioning style that helps you dig down to the real truth of your automatic thoughts to the deeper underlying core belief framework. The more precisely you can ask the following types of questions about your automatic thoughts, the more information you will gain from the answer:

1. What does this mean about me in this situation?

2. What does this mean about the world, my friends, my family?

3. What is the worst thing about this situation, thought, feeling? Why is this bad?

4. What might I believe about myself that would make this so upsetting? Why does this disturb me so much?

For example, Emily had the automatic thought, "She is only interested in herself," when her mother telephoned her to ask why she hadn't called in the last two weeks. She knew she felt annoyed and angered by her mother, but she wasn't sure why she felt more depressed after this event. The downward arrow technique helped her realize her core belief by persistently asking her to move deeper into herself to reach for the truth of this situation.

Emily's Downward Arrow

Automatic Thought

"She is only interested in herself."

(Emily notices she feels more depressed as she thinks this.)

↓

Downward Arrow

"What does this mean about me, that she is only interested in herself?"

"What does this mean about my mother?"

↓

Assumption

"It means she is not really interested in me."

"It means my mother doesn't know how to love me."

↓

Downward Arrow

"What is the worst thing about her not being
interested in me? Why is this bad?"

Assumption

"The worst thing about her not being
interested in me is that I feel rejected."

Downward Arrow

"What is it about feeling rejected that is so disturbing to me?

Core Belief

"I am unwanted."

You may notice that the downward arrow technique helps
Emily identify her automatic thoughts, assumptions, and core belief,
but it doesn't help her identify her primary strategy. To identify
your strategy, you need to ask yourself questions about your
behavior, not your thoughts. Typically, your behavior helps protect
you from the pain of feeling the core belief. For example, Emily
used the strategy of being pleasant to others to win friendships so
she could avoid feeling unwanted. The following questions can help
you see the behavioral strategies you commonly use:

1. How do I behave to keep myself feeling comfortable with
   myself and with others? If you are unsure of what you are
   doing, review activity and thought tracking as explained in
   chapter 3.

2. What am I afraid to do with others? (Be vulnerable, angry,
   tender, critical, etc.)

3. What feelings do I most want to avoid? How do I behave
   to avoid these feelings?

4. How do I behave to keep feeling safe or comfortable?

Shifting the Structure

As you become more familiar with your core belief framework, you now have the opportunity to challenge both the thoughts and behaviors that serve as the driving force in your everyday life. The easiest way to start shifting your core beliefs is to begin recognizing and challenging the automatic thoughts, because automatic thoughts are closest to the surface of your consciousness. Like the man sitting at the riverbank who doesn't see the groundwater but does see the fish swimming below the surface of the river. As you learn to challenge the automatic thoughts, you will become more skilled in seeing the underlying structure and will have more capacity to change the thoughts and feelings that make you prone to being depressed. Meditation helps you begin to observe your thoughts, and it significantly weakens their grip on your sense of well being.

Shifting or changing the core belief structure requires using the combined tools of CBT and meditation. When you understand your core beliefs you will be able to use the CBT skills of thought challenging to shift the belief. Furthermore, you can set up experiments that will ultimately give you new experiences to weaken the grip of the core belief. An example of how this can work is when Emily decided to tackle her fear that she was going to be fired from her job because she had the basic core belief that she was unwanted. To better understand the relationship between her moods, events, and automatic thoughts, Emily tracked these events on paper, using a 1 to 10 scale (see Emily's Automatic Thoughts on page 63). In one column she tracked her mood, with 1 being her best mood and 10 being her worst mood. In the other columns she tracked the events and automatic thoughts that contributed to her fluctuating moods. Because she had done the work with the downward arrow technique she had been able to recognize that she held the core belief that she was not wanted. Her use of mindfulness meditation had helped her recognize the many permutations that this core belief had in the automatic thoughts that she both watched travel through her mind and tracked on paper. She knew at some level that she had been doing a good job, as her boss had told her that her expertise was needed on another case, but nevertheless she was aware that she feared being fired because she held the deeper core belief that she was unwanted. She decided to challenge her core belief by asking her boss for an interim evaluation to determine if her work was up to par and to find out if there was any risk of her being fired. This was a bold step for Emily, and it forced her to review and evaluate her work for the last six months to prepare for the interim review. When the evaluation occurred she learned that she was perceived as a valuable team player and an asset to the firm. The boss appreciated her proactively asking for feedback.

Emily made a smart move when she decided to start by challenging her work situation and not her belief that her mother didn't want her. Why was this smart? When you start to challenge your core belief, you want to take moves that are small and likely to succeed, rather than go immediately to the most threatening and potentially stressful relationship or dynamic. After time and a series of positive experiences you will have more internal strength to take on relationships or issues where you typically feel vulnerable.

The Finger Pointing to the Moon

Have you ever been out in an autumn evening and had someone point to the rising moon? No doubt you did not confuse the finger pointing to the moon with the moon itself. Once you have seen the moon, the pointing finger is no longer necessary for the clear perception of the moon. The image of the finger pointing to the moon is a famous image in Zen, and it applies to working with your core beliefs. The danger in using the core belief framework is that we come to think of the framework as a hard structural reality. Our perception about what is authentic and true in our life gets understood through this particular structure. It's as though we forget to look at the moon, the true reality, and we only look at the finger pointing to the moon, the believed structure. The danger of this approach is that we come to believe that the pointing finger *is* the moon.

Once people have become very familiar with their core belief framework there can be a tendency to try to sort all their life experience into this framework so that their disparate experiences make structural sense. It is as though you pushed your life experience through a sieve with round holes, but really what fits is a sieve with square holes. While many times these frameworks can be useful and helpful, they are not always accurate for every situation. We have numerous core belief frameworks, not just one. It is quite possible for a different core belief to be activated, but because you are aware of one framework, you don't tend to look for a different, more accurate core belief. When forcing your life experience through a familiar framework you can narrow and restrict your life rather than opening to a different authentic life pattern. Should you find yourself doing this, return to the downward arrow technique to help you determine other possible core beliefs. Also, use your mindfulness practice to sit with your life experience and physically feel what is the truth of your life. When used effectively, the core belief model should be a powerful tool for liberation because it clarifies experience and helps you see the path toward more internal freedom.

Mindfully Moving into Your Core Belief

The grace of mindfulness combined with CBT is learning to sit, to just be with the complex framework of the core belief structure. Mindfulness emphasizes the clear seeing, understanding, and experiencing of all that makes up the core belief structure. Change occurs because awareness provides persistent erosion of the foundation of the framework. Rarely does the framework completely disappear, even in advanced students of meditation. However, the tangle that snarls people in the web of depression is, over time, so clearly seen and easily recognized that the web is no longer as tenacious, the strands can no longer readily pull you down into depression. Furthermore, cognitive therapy helps you learn to identify, challenge, and experiment with the distorted web of thoughts so that ultimately the core beliefs are modified, shifted, and changed.

Direct Experience

Freedom from depression comes from the direct experience of your core beliefs. The regular practice of mindfulness gives you the strength and fortitude to clearly perceive the framework of your core belief structure. Mindfulness also gives you the internal capacity to sit with and physically experience in your body the sensations that underlie this framework.

Some techniques in mindfulness meditation involve mental activity such as counting your breaths, labeling thoughts, or noting mind. These are important aspects of mindfulness practice, but the center of mindfulness is just experiencing. In sitting meditation this means feeling the sensations in your body and the environment as much as you can: the sensation of your body weight as you touch a cushion or the floor, the feel of the air on your skin, hearing the sounds in the room and beyond it, seeing the objects in your range of sight. Experiencing these things is very concrete in contrast to thinking, which takes you away from being aware of the physical reality inside and around you.

Of course, when we're absorbed in thoughts they seem much more real and certainly more important than the feel of the air on our arms! But our thoughts aren't more real than our bodies and environment. Our thinking mind finds this hard to accept because it is so contrary to our core beliefs. How can the feelings in my chest be more important than the "fact" that I am a terrible/fearful/inadequate person! This is why it's important in meditation to return from our thoughts to our physical experience over and over again. What "heals" us from our thinking mind is becoming aware a few seconds at a time of the physical reality that we're a part of. So working with core beliefs is not only coming to understand them intellectually, it is becoming aware of them in your body.

What does it mean to directly experience your core beliefs? It means simply being willing to let your attention move into your body so you can feel the quiver, the tension, and the many mildly unpleasant sensations that may accompany your automatic thoughts, assumptions, and core beliefs. These sensations are conditioned in your body, and the core belief structure is organized around the avoidance of experiencing them. When you gently let yourself experience the tension, the quiver, the empty feeling in the belly while also maintaining an awareness of the outside environment (so you don't get lost in fear of the physical sensations), you are softening your core belief framework. This process of coming back into the body, your home, is mindfulness. You are connecting to what is real for you in this moment, as opposed to a thought about what is real. You are not trying to wiggle away from the moment, change the pain, or fashion a new idea; rather, you are being present with the whole moment, with your life. This connection to the ground of your being loosens the tangle of depression, allows you to have a new relationship with yourself and realize a deeper unity with all that holds and surrounds you in this world.

Directly experiencing our physical reality is simple, but that doesn't mean it's easy. This is because our self-centered minds don't want to give up our core beliefs. Anything that threatens the supremacy of our core beliefs structures is frightening. Who would we be if not the person we think we are at our seemingly deepest levels? It is difficult for our minds to tolerate giving up the drama of core beliefs even for a few minutes. This is true even though the drama makes us miserable. That's why, as Joko Beck has said, we must be both patient and persistent. Direct experiencing is difficult but not impossible. We don't want to do it. We don't want to have to label the thought, "not wanting to do this." But when you can label the thought anyway and return even for a few seconds to your body, the core belief structures weaken.

Being patient in meditation grows from an increasing compassion for yourself. The harsh judgments may come quickly when we begin to do mindfulness work. "I'm no good at this," "This isn't going to work." But if you can return to your body—again, even for a few seconds—you build that muscle of awareness. The muscle of awareness shows you that at times, yes, this is hard, and no, you really don't want to do it, but returning is always available to you.

As you review this chapter on core beliefs it will be normal to try and figure out your core belief framework. This is quite natural and a good exercise. Let yourself use mindfulness to notice patterns in your life. Watch your thoughts and moods over the next weeks and months and ask yourself, "What is the driving belief under these thoughts and moods?" You can use the downward arrow technique to try to clarify these thoughts. Over time you will sift through your many life experiences and varying thoughts and a clear core belief structure will emerge. When you have the precise core belief, you will know that it is exact, as it will fit your life experience like a key in a lock. The key can open the door, and you will clearly begin to see the assumptions, strategies, and automatic thoughts that follow from your core belief. As you read the upcoming chapters on the relationship between thoughts, activities, and people to your mood, you will gain new insights into how these relate back to your possible core belief system.

5

understanding and changing depressed thinking

In the preceding chapters, you have learned to notice your thoughts, activities, and feelings. Many times these skills alone can bring about improvements in mood. However, this chapter provides you with skills to identify how your thoughts relate to your mood, and then how to change those thoughts.

Depression Changes Your Thinking

If you are feeling depressed, you may have noticed that your thinking is very different from times when you're not depressed. You might tend to remember sad things and have a hard time recalling times you were happy or felt good about yourself. You might find that you're more judgmental of either yourself or others or that you notice obstacles that you didn't previously see. If you have been depressed a long time, you might not even remember good things or a time when you weren't judgmental or critical.

Research shows that these types of thinking can be both a cause of depression and a result of depression. In particular, research has shown that some people with a history of depression may have a "latent cognitive vulnerability" that increases their risk for depression (Miranda and Persons 1988; Miranda, et al. 1998). What that means is that some people, when they feel fine, see things and remember things in pretty much the same way other people do. However, when something brings their mood down, their thinking takes on depressive characteristics (self-critical, biased, rigid) to a much greater extent than people who are not vulnerable to depression. This increase in depressive thinking may then increase the risk of further symptoms, leading to a downward spiral into depression.

There is some very good news, however. Zindel Segal and his colleagues did a study where they measured what happens when people received CBT (Segal, Gemar, and Williams 1999). They found that CBT appears to significantly reduce this vulnerability. Interestingly, they found that while medication was just as effective for treating depression, it didn't reduce the vulnerability. This may be part of the reason why people treated just on medication tend to get depressed again if they stop their medication.

What does this all mean for you? In this chapter, we are going to practice identifying depressive thinking and then changing it. By learning how to change depressive thinking, you both reduce your depression right now and potentially reduce your risk of future depressive episodes.

Catch It, Check It, Change It

To change a thought that worsens depression, you need to follow the three Cs: you first have to notice the thought (*catch* it), determine whether it is accurate or inaccurate (*check* it) and then, if it's inaccurate, generate a more accurate, helpful replacement thought (*change* it). The three Cs are an easy way to remember how to do this.

Whenever you find that you're feeling depressed (or some other emotion you want to understand), write down:

✦ The situation (for instance, "talking with my wife").

✦ The emotion you felt and how strongly you felt it on a scale from 0 (not at all) to 100 (extremely).

Now you are ready for the three Cs!

Catch It: Notice Your Thoughts When You Are Depressed.

The first step for changing your thinking is to notice your thoughts in specific situations. The thought tracking from chapter 3 is a great way to do that. The more quickly you pay attention to your thinking when you're feeling depressed, the more likely you'll be able to identify any problematic thoughts. Sometimes, it's hard to notice what you are thinking in a certain situation. When you run into trouble, remember the observing skills from chapter 3. Some things you can do to help are:

+ Try saying out loud what is going through your mind.

+ Name the emotion you're feeling, and then ask yourself what might you be telling yourself about the situation that would lead to this feeling.

+ Take three breaths with a mindful stance; just notice what is in your mind.

+ Try writing down what's going through your mind without editing.

If you try one or more of these approaches, it will increase the chance that you can catch what you're thinking. If you cannot identify your thoughts, you don't need to beat yourself up; just try again the next time you notice yourself having a painful emotion like sadness, anger, or fear. Remember that these are skills that take practice to learn.

Sometimes there will be more than one thought that's bothering you. It can be helpful to catch and write down all the thoughts you notice. However, when you start checking the thoughts, choose the thought that you think bothers you the most and start with that. Some therapists call this the "hot thought." (Greenberger and Padesky 1995). By focusing on the hot thought, it's easier to stay on target and possibly see some improvement in your mood.

Sometimes you may write down a thought, and as you look at it, you can't see why it's leading to the emotion. In this case, it can be helpful to ask yourself how the thought relates to your core beliefs.

Here's an example. One client reported that he felt really angry with himself and guilty when remembering his divorce. However, the first thought he reported was, "I did everything I could.

There was nothing I could have done differently." The therapist pointed out that it was not clear why this thought would lead to guilt and anger and wondered if there was another thought involved. The client then stated, "Well, since I did the best I could and it didn't work out, I should just get over it. I'm stupid for still carrying a torch for her." In this case, the original thought was not the one driving the current emotion, but rather a thought *about* the original thought.

Therefore, when you are catching thoughts, check to see if you can make sense of how they relate to the emotion you want to change. If the thought is not obviously related to the emotion, there might be another one that you've missed.

Check It: Is There Anything Wrong with This Thought?

Once you've noticed your thinking, you can check if there are any distortions in the thought.

Common Distortions

Aaron Beck, David Burns, and many other authors have identified several characteristics of depressive thinking. You can check the thought by asking yourself if it matches any of the types of thinking below.

Negatively biased. Not surprisingly, depressive thinking tends to focus more on negative outcomes, self-criticism, and past or future failures and losses. This is a problem, because when you focus on the negative, you tend to ignore the positive, and you don't see all the choices or options you might have. Examples include:

+ **Mental filter:** You only notice the negative (for example, getting job feedback and only noticing the criticisms).

+ **Discounting the positive:** You notice positive things, but twist them to be negative (like, "He only complimented me because he wants something").

+ **Emotional reasoning:** You believe that something is true because it matches how you feel (for instance, "I feel hopeless, therefore there is no point in looking for work"). Oftentimes depressed people will say, "I know it's not true, but it *feels* true" and then act on that feeling rather than on what they know in their head to be true.

These negative biases all stem from a negative core belief and related assumptions. The core belief leads to mental filters, because you tend to notice information that is consistent with your core belief and to ignore other information. When you do notice contrary information, your core beliefs lead you to twist it, causing you to discount the positives. Because the core belief feels true, and the emotions stemming from it feel true, you assume they accurately reflect reality and engage in emotional reasoning.

Overgeneralization. Depressive thinking tends towards generalities ("I failed") rather than specifics ("I got a C on the test"). You might have noticed that in chapter 3 we emphasized how important it is to be specific. When you think in generalities, it makes it hard to know where to make changes. For example, if you tell yourself, "I'm a failure," you will likely feel overwhelmed. On the other hand, telling yourself, "I did not get this job because I didn't have the right experience," helps you know what to do next (apply for jobs that match your experience; get more education).

"Name calling" is a particular type of overgeneralization. You describe yourself or others with labels, rather than specifying activities (for example, after losing a game, calling yourself a "loser" rather than saying, "I lost one game."). The problem with name calling is that the labels you use tend to stick in your head, and they are often easier to use than a more accurate description of the situation.

When you overgeneralize, you will find that you don't have many options. When you call yourself names, they often feel permanent and unchanging.

Personalizing. Whereas non-depressed people tend to blame situations and things for their mistakes, depressed people tend to blame themselves. If you personalize things, you may notice that you think mistakes you make reflect something innate about yourself rather than just being isolated occurrences. You might even feel guilty for things outside of your control. This is a problem because if you're blaming yourself for things that aren't in your control, you will feel bad and you won't be able to change the situation. If you can notice what is and what is not in your control, you can focus on what you can change and learn to live with what you cannot change. An example of this dynamic is active self-blame—blaming yourself for things that are not totally your fault, or are even totally out of your control (like hearing that a friend got injured in a car accident and thinking "If I were there, I would have prevented my friend from getting hurt").

Rigid thinking. Depressed thinking tends toward absolutes. ("There is no point in trying." "It will never work." "I always screw up.") When you think in absolutes, you reduce your options. If you believe things have to be just one way, you're setting yourself up for unhappiness. Rigid thinking is often referred to as "all or nothing" thinking. This is seeing situations as black or white, ignoring all the shades of gray in between. ("I did not get a perfect score on a test, so I failed.") This type of thinking is often associated with perfectionism. If you are using all-or-nothing thinking, you likely find yourself using absolute terms like "always," "never," "everything," and "nothing." You might do this just out of habit or as a way to emphasize a point. For example, you might say to yourself, "I never do anything right," really meaning, "I hate to make mistakes." The problem with the first statement is that it makes the situation sound and feel worse than it actually is, and that likely increases your depression.

Judgmental thinking. We all carry a whole lot of rules in our head about what is right and wrong and how things should be. Depression is associated with a tendency to focus on these rules and judge yourself and others as to whether they are living up to the rules. When you violate the rules (in other words, you don't do what you should) you beat yourself up emotionally (for instance, "I should not feel this way"). When other people violate the rules, you criticize or reject them. Because the thoughts associated with these judgements often included words like "should," "must," and "have to" we call them "should" thoughts for short.

Should thoughts add to depression because when you use them on yourself ("I should be a better wife"; "I should work harder") you tend to feel guilty. Although shoulds are intended to motivate, they actually can get in the way of you doing what you think you should because they make you feel depressed, and when you are depressed it's harder to do what you should! They also make your depression worse when you use them on things outside you. Thoughts like "people should be more polite" and "things were better in the old days" (a judgment that implies things now should be different) lead to frustration and provide no solutions.

Ruminating on these criticisms just makes you feel worse about the people and world around you.

Jumping to conclusions. Depression can lead to making assumptions about things that you cannot know for sure. Even though these assumptions may be wrong, it's easy to act as if they're true. The assumptions are guided by your core beliefs. There are two main kinds of assumptions:

✦ **Fortune telling:** Depression leads you to predict that bad things will happen in the future (like, "I will never get better").

✦ **Mind reading:** Depression may also lead you to assume you know what other people are thinking about you. When you're depressed, you are particularly likely to assume that they think negatively about you (for example, "No one cares").

Both of these thinking errors can be doubly destructive. First, they make you feel bad. Second, they prevent you from doing things that could improve your mood. If you assume things will go badly, you probably won't try (or you do try, but do so in a way that guarantees that things go badly). If you think people are thinking badly of you, you may end up acting in ways that in fact cause those people to treat you badly.

These different types of thinking can strongly contribute to your depression. However, by identifying the thoughts running through your mind you can then question whether they are potentially biasing your perceptions and increasing your depression. You can then identify thoughts that are more accurate and helpful, and that may lead to improved mood. You may notice that some of these categories overlap, and many thoughts can have several problems. For example, "I'll never get better" is fortune telling (predicting the future) and all or nothing thinking (assuming there will be no improvement). The next step we'll take helps you use this knowledge to come up with more accurate, helpful thoughts.

Changing your thoughts

Okay, you've caught your thoughts, and you've checked whether there are any problems with them. Now it's time to change those unhelpful thoughts.

There are several ways to change your thinking. Each approach has plusses and minuses. It is often good to try out many ways of looking at your thinking so that you can find the approach that works best for you.

Identify the Error and Correct It

If you find that you can identify the thinking error, sometimes just correcting that error can give you a more helpful thought. The sections below give hints on how to check each kind of thinking error.

Negatively biased thinking. If you have checked your thoughts and think there is a negative bias, it is helpful to ask several questions:

+ What information might I be ignoring?

+ Are there any positives here that I'm minimizing?

+ Am I twisting something to make it worse than it is?

+ Am I listening more to my emotions than to my brain?

If any of these questions are answered yes, then ask yourself what additional information you are ignoring (for example, What are the positives? How are you twisting things? What does your head say?). This can often be a simple way to take a new perspective and improve your mood.

Overgeneralization. If you think you are overgeneralizing, ask yourself:

+ Am I name-calling?

+ Can I describe the action or situation instead of name-calling?

+ Does the situation really mean that the label I'm using applies, or is this overgeneralizing?

+ Are there any situations in which the generalization I'm using is not true? Which?

+ How would I describe the situation so that someone who didn't know me would know exactly what happened?

These questions can help you get specific and break down the overgeneralizing. In particular, getting down to "just the facts" is really helpful when you are trying to recognize overgeneralizing in your thinking.

Personalizing. When you're personalizing, it is often helpful to step outside of yourself and take another person's perspective. You can do this in a couple of ways. Ask yourself:

+ How would a friend or someone I trust view the situation?

+ If people I cared about were telling themselves this, what would I tell them?

+ Am I taking responsibility for anything outside my control?

+ Am I ignoring or minimizing the responsibility of others?

The first two questions help you get some perspective. In a way, what they are saying is, "If I didn't believe my core belief, what would I tell myself?" The second two questions help you define the situation more accurately, taking a more complete perspective.

Rigid thinking. Changing rigid thinking requires filling in the gap. If you are using all-or-nothing thinking you can restate most things by trying to measure them. For example, rather than, "I choked on the test," you can state, "I got a 57 percent." It may not seem like a big improvement, but at least you got something right. Rather than saying, "Nothing ever goes my way," you can say, "This situation didn't go exactly how I wanted, but some parts worked out okay, and other things have worked out for me in the past." The point in challenging rigid types of thinking is to always look for the exceptions.

Judgmental/should thoughts. One of the best ways to examine judgments and should thoughts is to use mindfulness. Judgments are evaluating whether things are right or wrong. Mindfulness just describes how things are. By focusing on what is rather than how you think things should be, you can decide how to act given the reality of the situation.

This comes back to the theme that acceptance is not defeat. Some people feel that if they stop applying their judgments, they have endorsed or given in to the things they judge as wrong. Not at all. Rather, by acknowledging how things are, without judging, you can then make a choice about how you want to act, given your values. For example, rather than saying, "I should be a better father" you can describe the specific situation: "I spend no time with my child during the week and about an hour on the weekends." This acknowledges the situation, but also provides a baseline against which you decide to act. You might decide that you would like to increase the time that you spend with your child or else change what you do when you're with your child.

Another solution to shoulds about yourself is to rephrase them. Rather than focus on what you *should* do, describe to yourself the benefit of doing it. In the example above, rather than saying "I should be a better father," the person can focus on "If I spend an extra half hour a night with my kid, it will give his mom a break, it will make him happy, and I will feel better about myself." By focusing on the positives rather than the negatives, you will feel less depressed and are more likely to change your behavior.

Jumping to conclusions. When you notice you might be jumping to conclusions, you can correct this by checking out the assumptions. The following questions can be helpful:

✦ What assumptions am I making?

✦ What is my evidence?

✦ Are there any other possible explanations I'm ignoring? What are they?

✦ How do I know this will happen in the future?

✦ How do I know what he/she is thinking?

The answers you will often get is that you have no evidence or that you don't know. Generating alternative explanations is particularly important, because they may be much more positive and might improve your mood.

But what if your predictions or mindreading are right? One important approach to dealing with jumping to conclusions is the "Meatballs" strategy. This is particularly useful when what you fear or dread turns out to be true. This strategy is based on a comedy many years ago about kids at summer camp called *Meatballs.* In one scene the action switches back and forth between two camps. Both camps are preparing for an upcoming competition and are having big rallies. In the one camp, everyone is chanting, "We're number one!" In the other camp, everyone is chanting, "It just doesn't matter!"

The Meatballs strategy basically involves asking yourself, "If what I fear turns out to be true, so what?" Often you'll find that an event that you could get worked up about just doesn't matter that much in the big scheme of things. The Meatballs strategy just means asking, "How much does this really matter in the grand scheme of things?" If the answer is, "Not much," then you may find yourself feeling less anxious and depressed.

In addition to these approaches to checking unhelpful thoughts, it is often helpful to ask yourself how the problem thoughts relate to your core beliefs. In chapter 4, you worked on identifying a core belief that may influence your thinking. To change an unhelpful thought related to the core theme, ask yourself:

+ Is this thought consistent with my core belief?

+ If I did not believe the core belief, what would I tell myself instead of the current thought?

As you gather new alternative thoughts, check whether you have information that either supports or contradicts these thoughts.

Generating a New, More Helpful Thought

Once you've figured out what was wrong with the old thought, you can generate a new thought that is both more accurate and likely to help your mood. Below we give an example of how Bob used the techniques of the three Cs to come up with new, more helpful thoughts. You can use Bob's example to guide yourself through your own 3 Cs form. A copy of the form is in the appendix.

Bob notices that he is feeling down after forgetting to stop for groceries. He fills out his catch it, check it, change it form as follows:

Bob's Three Cs

Where and When: home, after forgetting groceries

Feelings (0-10): Embarrassed (8) Upset (6)

CATCH the thought (What I told myself)	CHECK It (What's wrong with this thought)	CHANGE It (What would be a better thought)
I'm an idiot.	Name calling and Overgeneralizing	One mistake does not make me an idiot. I had a busy day and got a lot done. It helps if I give myself some credit for that
Mary is going to be really angry.	Jumping to conclusions	I don't know that she will get upset. In the past, she has been understanding. Even if she gets upset, she usually gets over it fast.

When Bob first notices his feelings, he scores them on the 0 to 10 scale. He then writes down the thoughts he is noticing. He has several, but the two that bother him the most are, "I'm an idiot," and, "Mary is going to be really angry." He decides to check the "idiot" thought first, because he thinks it's the one that bothers him the most and it relates to the core belief, "I'm not good enough." In reading through the types of thinking errors, he notices that this seems like name calling and overgeneralization, and so he writes these down next to the thought. He then starts asking some questions to clarify, including:

Question: Instead of labeling, what is an accurate description of the situation?

Answer: I forgot one thing today, picking up the groceries.

Question: Would I call my wife an idiot if she did this?

Answer: No.

Question: Were there any extenuating circumstances?

Answer: Yes. It was a very busy day, and I had a lot on my mind.

After doing this exercise, Bob generates two thoughts that are more accurate, which he writes down in the "Change It" column:

✦ One mistake does not make me an idiot.

✦ I had a busy day and got a lot done. It helps if I give myself some credit for that.

Bob then decides he also wants to check the thought that Mary will be really angry. He again reviews the list of thinking errors and notices that this is jumping to conclusions. He then asks himself:

Question: How do I know she will be really angry?

Answer: I don't. Sometimes she gets annoyed when I forget things, but she usually doesn't get really angry. Even when she gets angry, she usually gets over it soon.

Having checked and changed each thought, Bob then goes back and examines his feelings. He finds that his embarrassment has dropped to "3" and his upset is down to "2." This suggests that the challenges are helpful.

Your Turn

Learning to catch, check, and change thoughts that contribute to depression is a central skill in CBT. There are two particularly helpful ways to start practicing these skills:

1. Schedule a time each day (like just after dinner) to review the day. Choose one situation from the day and fill out the three Cs form. After you fill out the Change It section, see if you think that the new thoughts are more helpful.

2. Keep a three Cs form with you. *Immediately* after a situation in which you have a negative feeling, fill it out. Check whether your mood improves by seeing if your scores on the negative feelings go down.

Developing Alternative Core Beliefs: The New You

One of the big difficulties that can arise from challenging your thoughts and questioning your core beliefs is that you then see the flaws of the core beliefs and want to replace them. Because let's face it, the core beliefs are there for a reason—they organize how you perceive yourself and everything around you. They are tools you use to help you try and achieve your goals and live up to your values. And they have worked for you at many times and places in your life. Changing such a central and important aspect of your being can feel like trying to create a whole new you.

Let Values Be Your Guide

We try and take the approach of not throwing the baby out with the bathwater. You have a set of values and beliefs that guide what you do. These are often based on religious teaching, your family traditions, or other important influences you've had in your life. One way to think about core beliefs is that they are attempts to get you to fit with these general values.

Bob had been raised in a family that valued hard work, honesty, and humility. To help him achieve these values, his parents were quick to point out when he was not living up to those values. As he grew up, however, Bob did not perceive the criticism as an attempt to help him become a better person, but rather as the message that he wasn't good enough. This perception was the basis for his core belief. At this point, although he was fulfilling the values he had learned, he continued to feel that he wasn't good enough.

In Bob's case, the general values are not the problem. Most people will agree that hard work, honesty, and humility are good things. The problem was that his core belief, despite helping him to achieve his values, also made him vulnerable to depression. So what to do? The following are some steps that can help you generate a new core belief that is consistent with the values that you want in your life.

First, think about your values. This is a big task and means asking some big questions. Some questions that you can consider are:

✦ What do I value most in my life? How does my life reflect those values?

✦ What are the characteristics I value in myself? How does my core belief support or detract from theses values?

✦ What makes people valuable? Do all people have some innate value, or does their value vary based on characteristics or the things they do?

✦ What are the characteristics I value in others and the characteristics that I want to have in myself? Think about physical, mental, emotional, moral/ethical features.

✦ What are my beliefs about the nature of life and death? What do I think is the point to life here on earth?

It can be helpful to write your answers down. Many times we have some vague ideas about our values, and both asking and answering such questions can go a long way toward clarifying them.

Next, figure out the costs and benefits of the core belief in terms of achieving your values. You can do this just by drawing two columns and writing the benefits and costs down. In Bob's example, he notices that his core belief is beneficial when it pushes him to succeed, but he pays for it with depression that probably gets in the way of living up to his values.

Consider another example. One patient in our clinic had the belief, "I am innately flawed. There is something horribly wrong with me." Based on this belief, he tended to be very unassertive, accept criticism unquestioningly, and end up in relationships where he was treated quite badly. He would sacrifice and give to others but would not take care of his own needs. He also felt that because of his flawed nature, he deserved to be punished.

This patient was also a very religious Christian. His therapist, a trainee in our clinic who came from a different country and religious background, knew very little about this man's spiritual beliefs and asked the patient to fill her in on his Christian values. When he got to the part about God loving everyone and that we are made in God's image, the therapist asked, "So why do you have to beat yourself up? If you believe God loves you and made you in his image, doesn't that mean that you are a worthwhile person just like everyone else?" This stopped the patient, and over the next few weeks, he started to recognize that his core belief ignored a big part of his values. When he asked himself whether God would agree with his core belief, he concluded that God would agree that he was flawed, but no more than anyone else. He also believed that God would love him anyway and support him, but not punish him. He started to act more assertively, and his mood started to improve.

In a different example, a patient who was an atheist had the core belief, "I am worthless," and held the assumption that, "If I am productive at my job, I might have some worth." When he suffered a series of health problems that prevented him from working he became depressed and even suicidal, stemming from the assumption, "If I can't work, I'm worthless." When he explored his values, he noted how critical he felt it was to make the most of life, because there is nothing else. In a way, this was very consistent with his value of respecting productivity. However, when we discussed how he viewed others who were unable to work, he said that he didn't think that they were totally worthless or should all kill themselves but rather should find other ways to contribute. While he continued to feel that productivity and contributing were important, he challenged the assumption that work was the only form of productivity, telling himself, "I do have things to share (knowledge, experience) that others may find helpful." With this revised assumption he started spending more time with his teenage grandson, talking about everything from car repair to World War II. The experience of sharing his knowledge was rewarding for both him and his grandson and led to him feeling less depressed.

Your thought challenging also helps you identify conflicts between your core beliefs and your values. Stepping back and asking if the core belief is consistent with your values is a great way to start challenging core beliefs.

Build from Your Values Up

Having started to challenge a dysfunctional core belief, you will need a new, more accurate one. Often, it's helpful to build it on what you can agree is true, that is, what you hold as your values (regardless if you currently achieve them). In the example above, the patient started working on a core belief that did not ignore the values he felt good about. The new core belief he came up with was, "I'm someone who cares about others and enjoys caring for others." He felt this was accurate—it described himself, endorsed his values, and did so in an encouraging way.

In generating new core beliefs, take the following things into account:

✦ Try to create a core belief that does not contain thinking errors such as those in chapter 5.

+ Frame your belief in the positive.

+ Base the belief on your values.

+ Acknowledge the basic truth that we are flawed and sometimes don't achieve our ideals.

+ Remind yourself of evidence that disputes the old core belief and supports the new core belief.

Unfortunately, just generating a new core belief does not make the old one go away, nor does it mean that you will automatically believe the new belief. It is very helpful to track how strongly you believe each in different situations. For example, when practicing mindfulness, you can use the labeling and noting skills to recognize thoughts that are consistent with either the old or new core belief. You can also conduct experiments. If you think of an action you would take based on the old core belief as your control condition, the experiment is to do something acting as if the new core belief is true. Let's look at how Bob does this.

Bob developed a new core belief of, "I am a guy who strives to be honest and hardworking. These things are important to me, but they don't define my worth. I'm as valuable as anyone else, even if I don't always succeed at my goals." He didn't believe it very strongly, but tried it out in several situations. In situations that he would usually interpret as meaning he wasn't good enough, he would ask himself how he would feel with the new core belief and found that he would generally be less depressed. He also found that he liked thinking about himself as someone who valued hard work (which he did feel was true) rather than thinking of himself as someone who wasn't good enough.

His new core belief was tested by his wife. The next time that she asked him to take time off from work, he assertively told her that getting the work done was important to him, and they made other arrangements to help her out. His old core belief would have him complying with his wife's request, leaving him feeling guilty and angry about failing at work.

Your new core belief can be a very helpful tool for generating alternative thoughts that work for you. Asking yourself, "Am I thinking with the old core belief or new core belief?" and, "What would the new core belief say or do?" can be a quick shorthand for challenging and changing the distorted beliefs, assumptions, and strategies stemming from your old core beliefs.

The Importance of Thoughts

By catching your thoughts, checking their accuracy, and then changing them, you can improve your mood in the immediate situation. In addition, by changing thoughts that interfere with your activities, you can improve your functioning and your interactions with people. As you go through the process of changing your thoughts, you may start to change your core beliefs. Throughout the rest of this book we will continue to refer back to thought challenging as the foundation upon which CBT is built.

6

activities and mood

The preceding chapter focused on thinking and mood. This one addresses activities and mood. In this chapter, you will learn how your activities can both directly and indirectly improve your mood. Chapters 5 and 6 compliment each other because when you work on your thinking, it will probably influence your activities, and when you increase your activities, it will often change your thinking. In fact, one of the most important roles that activities can play is to help you gather evidence that changes unhelpful beliefs.

Why the Focus on Activities?

Activities are a powerful component of CBT for several reasons. First, pleasant and/or rewarding activities by their very nature improve our mood. Think about the last thing you did that was just for fun. If you can't think of anything recent, try to think back farther. What we know is that people who are depressed often stop doing rewarding, fun things. This could be due to reduced energy, negative thoughts ("there's no point, I won't enjoy it"), or loss of opportunities (like job loss, health problems interfering, not enough time). However, increasing pleasant activities improves mood. In fact, some studies have suggested that just increasing pleasant activities alone, without even trying to change thinking, is as effective at reducing depression as doing CBT with both increasing activity and thought challenging (Jacobson et al. 1996). There is even some evidence that simply doing more activities scheduling leads to positive changes in thinking (Zeiss, Lewinsohn, and Muñoz 1979)!

Activities as Experiments

Why would it be that activity scheduling alone improves thinking? One possibility is that increasing activities actually gives you chances to challenge thoughts without even realizing it. For example, if you avoid doing things, you might start feeling guilty, thinking, "I'm lazy." Going out and doing something will provide you with evidence that you're not lazy. If you feel incompetent and predict that you will fail at something new, trying that new activity will either show you that your predictions are wrong or that, even if you're right, failing may not be as big a deal as you might think.

Each of these examples is an experiment—you test a belief and determine whether it is accurate. In the previous chapters you learned to identify core beliefs that may be playing a role in your depression. You have also learned to use mindfulness skills to observe your thinking, emotions, and physical sensations. Now, you can take this knowledge and do experiments to help you truly test whether the negative beliefs you hold about yourself are true or false.

So activities can both increase your mood directly and start helping you change how you think. In addition, you can engage in activities that lead to new skills and abilities that give you more options in your life. Reading this book is an example, where you have the chance to learn both about CBT and mindfulness and how to work with these techniques. Mindfulness skills are another example of a new activity that can both be rewarding in itself and also provide a new ability that gives you a whole new way to experience your life. The more choices you have, the more likely you can choose a path that is not depressing.

Learning new skills can be particularly important when you have lost the ability to do things you used to enjoy. Many of the people we work with at the San Diego VA have health problems that prevent them from doing what previously gave them pleasure, whether it was work or hobbies. In these situations, it's often very helpful to come up with either a new way to be involved with the old activity or a totally new activity. An example could be a woman who had loved gardening, but because of a back injury was unable to work in her garden. It was becoming overgrown, and she began feeling sad for the loss of the activity and guilty that her beautiful garden was such a mess. Rather than giving up, she could have gotten involved in teaching a child about gardening (such as her own daughter or being part of a "big sister" program). While we have changed this example to protect patient privacy, several of our patients who can no longer do valued activities have learned that teaching that skill can be a whole new reward.

In addition to learning a new skill or teaching an established skill, many activities can simply improve your general environment. Consider the gardening example. If the woman shows her daughter how to garden, the improved garden will be more pleasant to look at. Even something as simple as replacing a washer in a dripping faucet can improve the environment, as well as feel constructive.

Activities don't always result in a finished product, like a cleaned up house with no leaking faucet. Sometimes the result of an activity is not visible from the outside, but is something you feel on the inside. For example, getting some fresh air with a brief walk in a park can be a nice break and can help you feel more alert and energetic. Chapter 9 of this book will help you consider the benefits of exercise as an activity.

Beyond all these benefits, many activities involve dealing with people. Humans are social animals, and interactions with others can be our most powerful emotional experiences. The next chapter will focus particularly on interpersonal relationships and activities.

Hopefully you are in agreement that there may be some benefit to increasing rewarding activities, or at least you're willing to test it out. The next section provides some guidelines for successfully increasing the rewarding activities in your life. You may notice a pattern similar to that for thoughts. We are first going to *catch* the current activities in your life, *check* how those activities (or lack thereof) influence your mood, and then learn how to *change* those activities. You may decide to add new ones, decrease unhelpful ones, or change how you do things.

Evaluating Activities

The first step in understanding your activities is to figure out what you are currently doing. When you're depressed, you likely have thoughts that get in the way of your having an objective view of your activities, (for instance, "I don't do *anything*," or "I do way too much and have no time for fun"). To really get a sense of your activities, it is helpful to spend a week just tracking what you are doing using the activity tracking approach from chapter 3. This exercise helps you answer the following questions:

✦ What do I do that improves my mood? What things make my mood worse?

✦ What is my schedule like? Are there times that I can schedule rewarding activities?

✦ Am I taking on more than I can schedule in my week? Where might I need to cut back? Can I reorganize things to give myself some free time?

Based on what you learn, you can start increasing rewarding activities, and if possible, decreasing activities that make your mood worse. Consider Bob's tracking experiment.

When he tracked his activities, Bob noticed that he had enjoyed lunch with some friends, even though he hadn't really wanted to go. He noticed that his thoughts beforehand had been, "I have nothing to say," and, "This will be really awkward." However, when he was at lunch, he really enjoyed the food and was able to talk to one guy about a new car he had bought. Bob decided to test whether spending time with people might improve his mood. He decided to schedule lunch two days during that week with coworkers he liked. Bob then had the thoughts, "No one would want to have lunch with me," "I'll be wasting time—I shouldn't take a lunch break," and "I have too much to do." He challenged these thoughts by saying "Someone might want to have lunch—I can't know if I don't ask," "I wouldn't hold a lunch break against a coworker. Heck, it's a legal right," and "If I have to, I can stay late for a half hour to make up work."

Bob then asked a coworker if he wanted to grab lunch the next day. The coworker agreed. Bob rated his mood on the day when he had lunch with his friend and compared it to the days he didn't. He also checked his thoughts. He found that he enjoyed the lunch, that he and the coworker had plenty to talk about, and that he actually didn't have to stay late to finish up.

What Is the "Right" Activity?

In this last example, Bob knew at least one thing, going to lunch, would probably improve his mood. If you have been depressed for a while, or if you're facing certain challenges (health problems, money worries, lack of friends), it may be hard for you to think of rewarding activities to do. Two things might be getting in the way. First, you simply may not remember fun things. Second, you might think of an activity but then discount the idea (for example, "I could visit Amy—but no one wants to be around someone depressed like me").

Reminding Yourself of Pleasant Activities

First, let's think about ways to fix the first problem, forgetting fun things. In your notebook, write down any activities that you enjoy doing now or that you enjoyed doing in the past. Also write down at least three activities that you have not done but that sound fun to you. While you do this, if you find yourself discounting an activity, just ignore the criticisms and continue to write down items. A reasonable goal is to have a list of ten items that you think could be rewarding. If you come up with more, all the better.

After reviewing the list, ask yourself if there are any activities you used to do that you don't do any more. Ignore why you do not do them for now. Use your mindfulness skills to nonjudgmentally observe your thoughts but not react to them. For example, you want to take note of a discounting thought like, "I used to go to movies but can't anymore because I have no one to go with." Notice the thought but continue to add "going to the movies" to your activity list. If you are still having problems coming up with ideas, ask either friends or family. This can be helpful both in reminding you of things you forgot and in letting them know you're interested in doing things. When you are depressed people around you might assume that you don't want to be bothered. But if you reach out, it increases the likelihood others will reach back to you.

Stop Discounting, Start Testing

Now is the time to deal with the second part, the discounting. Read through your list, and identify your top three activities and plan to do them in the next week. As you do so, you're likely going to have thoughts about each one. If those thoughts are going to stop you from trying an activity, you can apply the skills learned in the last chapter to these thoughts. Ask yourself:

✦ Am I ignoring any upside, just thinking about problems and ignoring that I might feel better?

✦ Am I blowing any of the potential problems out of proportion? Am I distorting how bad the problems might be? (for example, "I have no money, so I can't do anything," vs., "I have thirteen dollars for the next week that I can spend," or, "I can do something that doesn't cost anything")?

✦ Am I jumping to conclusions? Am I assuming that I won't enjoy it or something will go wrong? If so, what's my evidence that these predictions are true?

You can use these questions to keep an open mind. Examine each thought about each activity until you have decided on at least one to try in the next day.

The Pleasure Predicting Experiment

One of the best ways to deal with discounting is to set up an experiment. Oftentimes, the discounting thought is something like, "It won't help," or, "I won't feel any better, so it's not worth doing." If you're having this thought, do the following experiment:

✦ Write down how much you think you will enjoy the activity, from 0 to 10 (for instance, "walking on beach, 10").

✦ Go and do the activity.

✦ Immediately after doing the activity, write down how much you actually did enjoy the activity.

If you find that your prediction was worse than reality, you now know that you are better off doing things even if you think they won't help. If your prediction was much better than reality, you might be setting yourself up for disappointment by having unrealistic expectations.

Doing Pleasant Activities

Now, if you have decided to try an activity to improve your mood, you can take steps to increase the likelihood that this will indeed be helpful. Each of the following are helpful ways to increase the chance that you'll do something and that you will benefit from it.

Figuring out What To Do First: Activity Hierarchies

Once you have identified things that you would like to try, you may need to break them down into smaller parts to make them manageable. We call this developing an activity hierarchy. What this means is that you plan out steps, from the simplest to the hardest.

Hierarchies are helpful for several reasons. Sometimes your initial goal may seem unreachable, and in fact, it might be. For example, if you have never gone jogging before and then try to run a marathon, you will likely fail. It seems pretty obvious that you need to train and work up to a marathon. Almost all other tasks can be seen in the same way. A hierarchy can allow you to develop the skill and the stamina necessary to achieve your goal. And importantly, simply by developing this hierarchy, you will be doing something on the way to your goal, rather than doing nothing and feeling worse.

Another reason hierarchies are important is that they allow you to test unhelpful beliefs that might be interfering with achieving your goals. Thoughts like, "I won't enjoy it," "I can't do it," "It's too much effort," and others can all be checked by starting out at an easy level. Think about another running example. You might want to do twenty to thirty minutes of aerobic exercise three to four days per week. Negative, blocking thoughts might come up when you think about running for thirty minutes, especially if you've never run before or if you have not run for a long time. However, one could develop a hierarchy that involved running for ten minutes the first day, and then increasing a minute a day for a month. By the end of the four weeks, if you run three days per week, you would be running for twenty-two minutes. You would also have tested whether running was enjoyable and worth the effort. Even if you decide that running isn't worth the effort, you have demonstrated that you can set up and test a hierarchy.

If you also have anxiety that leads you to avoid some activities, a hierarchy is a great way for you to start making progress. In fact, CBT therapists treating anxiety pioneered the use of activity hierarchies. By breaking down a feared activity (like driving on a freeway) into smaller components (driving past an onramp, driving up an onramp and off the next offramp, going two on-ramps, etc.) you can get used to the feared activity in small steps that reduce how anxious you feel. By actually doing the feared step several times, you will likely find that you are less anxious. You can then move on to the next step of the hierarchy, while gaining confidence that you can face your fears.

To design a hierarchy to increase activities, first choose the activity. Second, figure out what your goal is (what you want to do), and decide on a series of steps that can help you get there. When you consider steps, keep an open mind. Sometimes you might have thoughts that criticize your plan ("I shouldn't have to do this"; "This is stupid"). Use your mindfulness to notice that these thoughts are just thoughts, and then continue with your plan.

Scheduling Activities

If you just say, "I will go jogging sometime" you are far less likely to do it than if you say, "I will go jogging Wednesday at six o'clock, when I get home." The more specific the plan, the better. You also increase the chance that you will do something if you let other people in on your plan, and particularly if you schedule the activity with someone (however, don't let not having someone to do the activity with you stop you from doing it!). Effective scheduling requires the following materials:

+ A calendar (either paper or handheld computer)

+ A pencil with an eraser to write in your calendar

And you need to take the following actions:

+ Scheduling both your responsibilities and your entertainment in the calendar

+ Looking at your calendar each day

As with all things in this book, we encourage you to experiment and come up with a system that works for you. Beware of thoughts like, "I can keep it all in my head," or, "I shouldn't have to write it down, I should remember it," which are great ways to short-circuit your planning. Other thoughts might be that this is too much of a hassle or that it's too complicated. If you're having thoughts that interfere with doing things, write them down and check them out.

Did It Help?

Curiously, one of the big challenges of benefitting from activities is actually noticing the benefits. You will find that you remember and notice the benefits better if you write them down. Remember that when you're depressed, it's hard to remember positives and easy to remember negatives. Sometimes depressed people don't notice that an activity has helped them feel better. In chapter

3 you learned to use a weekly activity schedule to track what you do and to rate how it affects your mood. By tracking your activities you can help remind yourself of the benefits of your activities. In addition, if some activities aren't helpful, you can cut your losses once you've tried them a couple of times and move on to something else.

Bob's Story

One thought that got in the way of Bob asking a friend to join him for lunch was, "I have nothing to say." It was related to a more general thought of, "People find me boring," which Bob realized related to a core belief, "I'm not good enough." Bob thought about this as a hypothesis. He realized that if he thought of going out to lunch as his experimental condition and staying in the office as the control condition, he could test how much he enjoyed going out to lunch and whether his mood was better afterwards. He also could test whether he had anything to talk about by just noticing how the conversation went.

Bob rated his mood at the end of lunchtime both on the days he went out with a friend and the days he stayed in his office. He also paid attention to whether he had anything to say at lunch. In looking at his data, he realized that he did enjoy going to lunch with his coworker, and enjoyed it quite a bit more than staying in the office. He could then reject his original hypothesis and come up with a new one, "I usually feel better when I go to lunch with other people." He then thought about the second hypothesis, "I have nothing to say." He realized that he had talked during lunch, and he and his coworker seemed to be enjoying the break. He therefore rejected the second hypothesis as well and told himself, "I have something to say, and I was not so boring that the other guy didn't enjoy himself. At least I did well enough." In this way Bob was able to weaken his core belief of, "I'm not good enough," with the evidence that he felt better when going to lunch with a coworker and that he could interact with that person reasonably well.

Don't Just Do It—Do It and Learn from It

In the CBT model, activities can play a critical role in improving your mood and in changing your thinking. Activities both directly improve your mood and help you gather evidence to challenge beliefs that interfere with your mood. You may want to review and try the following activity-related exercises from this chapter:

✦ Create a list of activities that you think might be beneficial.

✦ If you question whether you can do an activity, break it down into parts in a hierarchy.

✦ Complete a weekly activity schedule so you can identify current rewarding activities and times when you can schedule additional activities.

✦ Using your weekly activity schedule (or your own personal calendar, if you have one), schedule in some additional rewarding activities. Consider starting with some easy activities or the first step in a hierarchy of a more difficult activity.

✦ Think about your core belief, and see if you can choose an activity that might help you test that core belief.

✦ Continue examining your thoughts as you start working on activities. You can use the thought-challenging skills from the preceding chapter to increase the chance that you'll get your activities done. You can use your activities to get evidence that challenges the thoughts that make you depressed.

7

people and your mood

No One Is an Island:
The Importance of Others

Nearly every theory of depression emphasizes the effect of people on mood. Have you ever noticed that being with some people makes you feel happier while interactions with others lead to you feeling anxious, depressed, or angry? The effect of one person on your mood changes in different situations. As you are learning to notice your thoughts and activities, you might also notice that many of the most powerful ones have to do with other people. Not surprisingly, people are important for several reasons. As you grew up, it was your relationship with your parents and the people around you that contributed to the core beliefs you now hold. Now, this does not mean that your current depression is the fault of those who raised you; the point is that how you think now has been learned from how you have dealt with people throughout your life. As you grow up, you learn to judge yourself based on how you are judged and how you see those around you act. You learn to act in a way that increases the chance that the people in your life will treat you well and decreases the chance that you'll be hurt or punished. The skills you develop in an attempt to cope with the world around you depend on two things. First, your basic temperament will shape whether you are you generally anxious or relaxed, impulsive or methodical. These traits predispose you to doing some things more than others (e.g., an impulsive person might ask for something they want whereas a more laid-back person might not). Second, your family, friends, and the culture around you have rules and standards, some obvious, some not, that define what is right and wrong, what gets rewarded and punished. We all face a balancing act of matching our natural inclinations (temperament) to the demands and expectations of the world around us.

Why do people so strongly influence how you view the world? Because they are a huge source of both rewards and punishments. Very few of us could survive without some sort of interaction with others. If you think about your own experience, some of your best and worst memories probably have to do with other people, whether they're about first love or a painful rejection, being told you succeeded at something or accused of failure.

Since people can be such a powerful source of both good and bad experiences, they become very important in our lives. When you are depressed, it can affect your relationships in several ways. You might withdraw to avoid more pain. You could reach out to people for help, feeling that you can't take care of yourself. You may become angry or irritable because you feel people in your life have let you down. You may become anxious, fearing you may lose support that you need now more than ever.

Depression can often stem initially from an interpersonal crisis. The loss of a loved one is one of the most powerful life events in terms of leading to depression. In addition, marital or relationship conflict is strongly associated with depression. When married couples have a significant conflict, the likelihood of depression in at least one partner is twenty-five times higher than in couples without conflict (Weissman 1987). In addition to these examples, you may notice other situations where relationships can contribute to the start of depression. Work relationships, for example with a demanding or critical boss, can make you feel much worse about yourself. You could potentially feel powerless in the face of a superior. Friendships can also be a source of stress if the friend is demanding or critical.

While your depression can influence how you react to people in many ways, the flip side is that you can challenge and conquer the depression with the help of people. Our goal in this chapter is to help you apply the skills you have learned so far for changing your thinking and actions to dealing with people. You will then learn skills that will help you to build and maintain supportive relationships, as well as ways to improve problematic ones.

Thinking and People

In previous chapters you learned how core beliefs lead you to certain assumptions and strategies that may contribute to your risk for depression. These patterns lead to automatic thoughts in response to your experiences, thoughts that are driven by your underlying core beliefs and assumptions. If you review the core beliefs in chapter 4, you will find that your relationships with people are a big part of what core beliefs are all about, and much of what is happening with depression centers around how you deal (or don't deal) with other people. For someone who has a core belief of being worthless or unlovable, it is other people who will often be the most powerful source of evidence that either supports or disputes these beliefs.

The first thing we will ask you to do in this chapter is pay attention to the automatic thoughts that arise for you when you're dealing with different people. The following exercise is designed to help you assess any thoughts that may have an important effect on your relationships with people.

Using Your Three Cs

Please fill out a "Three Cs" form each day for one week. Start today! Each day, choose a situation that has something to do with other people. It could be an interaction with someone (like talking with a coworker), or it could be something that makes you think about other people, like music that reminds you of a friend. Record your emotions in the "feeling" section, and in the "catch it" section write thoughts that occur during this situation that are specifically about people. As you complete the forms, pay attention to how your thoughts are related to your mood. For this exercise, you do not have to change the thoughts; the goal is to first notice the themes that come up when you deal with people.

At the end of the week, review the thoughts that you wrote down. Notice how they might relate to the core beliefs you recorded in chapter 3. It is a good idea to actually write out the thoughts on a new piece of paper and group them together by themes. Once you've done this, you may notice important patterns. What you are likely to find is that your thoughts about people, and particularly those very close to you, produce stronger emotions than thoughts about other things. In addition, you may find that most of the thoughts you have that affect your mood are about other people.

So what are some of the differences in dealing with the thoughts you have about people and those you have about other things (like your job, money, your own actions, possessions, etc)? There are several types of thinking errors that are primarily involved in dealing with people. In particular, we will focus on mindreading, shoulds, and name-calling, looking at how to spot them and what to do about them.

Mindreading

Mindreading, in particular, is specific to people (well, and pets; my cat just sat on my computer keyboard as I wrote this, and the thought that popped into my mind was, "He's annoyed 'cause I haven't paid much attention to him."). Mindreading occurs when you assume, without getting supporting evidence, that you know why a person did something. Why is mindreading a problem? Because when you're depressed, or when you have a powerful core belief activated about others, your mindreading is likely biased and often wrong.

Consider Bob again, who has the core belief, "I'm not good enough." His core belief leads him to devalue his accomplishments. This led to problems for Bob when dealing with other people. If someone complimented him, he would have mindreading thoughts like, "They're just saying that to make me feel good." (This is similar to what Freud called *projection*—you project your beliefs about yourself onto someone else, and assume they think about you the way you think about yourself.) As you can imagine, if this is how you consistently react to people, it's not going to help you make strong, trusting relationships.

How to Stop Mindreading

So what can you do about these thoughts you have relating to other people? To check mindreading, you first need to ask yourself, "How do I know that is what they're thinking?" or, "How do I know that is why they did that?" Asking those questions with my cat, I notice that I actually don't know that he is annoyed. You can also ask whether there is an alternative explanation for the behavior. I know my cat likes warm places. He might try to sit on the keyboard because it is warm. I also know that he is not very bright and often sits down on warm places that could be dangerous. So, rather than assume that he is annoyed with me, I can give him the benefit of the doubt.

Now when you are dealing with people rather than cats, you have the advantage of being able to ask them why they did what they did. This can be the most direct way to challenge your mindreading. One problem here is that you could just continue mindreading and discount any answer they give you.

Here are some things you can do to check out mindreading.

Get specific. In the example above with Bob, he could ask for clarification. When he received a compliment, he could make sure he understood what the other person means.

Mike: Hey Bob, changing the billing was a good idea.

Bob: (Mindreading by thinking, "He's just saying that"): Well, it may end up making things harder in the long run.

Mike: Jeez, can't you take a compliment?

See how much better it works when Bob gets specific and clarifies what's being said?

Bob: (Testing mindreading by checking automatic thought): I'm glad you're happy. What in particular do you like about the new system?

Mike: I think the effort up front will make things run more smoothly down the road.

And here's another tactic.

Bob: (Testing mindreading by being assertive and acknowledging doubts): I'm glad you like it Mike, but I worry that you are maybe ignoring some of the downsides of the new system. Have you considered the extra time it might take?

Mike: Sure, but I think in the long run it will pay off. What the heck, it's worth a try!

Or Bob could simply strive to accept the compliment at face value while challenging his mindreading tendency.

Bob: (Internally challenging mindreading by thinking, "Hey, I might think he doesn't mean it, but I have no evidence that's the case"): I'm glad you like it Mike.

Any of these approaches (clarifying, being assertive and acknowledging doubts, and internally challenging mindreading) are likely to be less depressing and produce a better interaction with

Mike than the first. In particular, the approaches that test the mindreading actually provide a chance to get more accurate information. In the first case, by asking for specifics, Bob sees if Mike has really thought things through. In the second case, Bob shares his feelings and gets a chance to check out his concerns more explicitly.

What if your fears are accurate? This is a good place to consider the Meatballs strategy from chapter 5. Consider again the example above:

Mike: Hey Bob, changing the billing was a good idea.

Bob: I'm glad you like it Mike, but I worry that you are maybe ignoring some of the downsides of the new system. Have you considered the extra time it might take?

Mike: Well, yeah, I think that could be a big problem, and I'm not sure that it will make sense for us to keep doing it this way.

Bob: Well, what do you want to do at this point?

In this case, Bob finds out that Mike wasn't as positive as he first presented. Rather than this being a tragedy, they can now try and work out the system together.

Mindful practice can help you start having enough distance from your experiences to practice the Meatballs strategy. By first stepping back and noticing your thoughts and noticing your mood in relationship to your thoughts, you can then ask yourself, if you choose, whether you want to stay with those thoughts, and ponder the change if you let them go.

Shoulds

Another type of thought that occurs a great deal when interacting with other people is "should" thoughts. In Bob's case, he might react to a compliment with the thought, "They should know better. Can't they see how badly I did this?" and end up feeling annoyed rather than happy. Should thoughts are really just a type of judgmental thinking. People use shoulds when they perceive that some rule or norm has been broken. Oftentimes, someone like Bob uses shoulds on himself ("I should do better") as well as those around him ("If she had any sense, she would give up on me").

Fixing Shoulds

Should thoughts are also quite responsive to mindfulness. Mindfulness is all about being present and being open to what is. You don't have to like it, and you don't have to want it to be that way, but being mindful is noting how things are (including your thoughts, feelings, and actions and the actions of the people in your life) without judging. Shoulds are, by definition, judgments. In fact, if you're having trouble with mindful practice, you might pay attention to whether there are should thoughts floating around that are leading you to be judgemental rather than mindful. If there are, just notice them and return to being mindful.

Particularly in relationship to other people, you can start modifying your shoulds by describing what is happening rather than what you think *should* have happened.

Consider Emily, whose mother did not return her call. Emily might have some should thoughts like:

✦ She should have called me back.

✦ She should be more interested in me.

✦ I must be doing something wrong. I should be a better daughter.

Practicing her mindfulness, Emily might take a few moments and describe the immediate situation to herself as it enters her awareness, returning attention to her breath as she chooses to: "I am in my home, in my living room, sitting near the phone. I am having thoughts that my mother should call, and that I should be a better daughter. As these thoughts move through me, my mood becomes angry and sad. At this moment, my mother is not calling. I can choose to listen to the thoughts, or I can accept that she has not called and decide how I want to be, given this fact."

By practicing mindfulness in this moment, Emily can distance herself from the should thoughts and make choices about how to react. By practicing moving her attention between her breath and her thinking and observations, she develops the option to listen to the thinking or not. This is quite a different experience than we often have, where the thoughts come up and we just accept them as true and react to them as if they are true.

A related but simpler approach is just to rephrase shoulds to describe how things *are* rather than how things should be. When you do this, it often gives you more options. Rather than striving to change things to how they should be (which is often impossible, particularly with past actions), you can decide what to do given how things are.

Emily might do the following. Instead of saying, "She should have called me back," she can rephrase this to, "She didn't call me back." This just describes the situation without judgement. Emily might be still unhappy, but by first accepting the situation, she can make some choices about how to respond without getting tied up in what her Mom should or should not have done.

"Ok, she didn't call. I am pretty disappointed, but I can either call her myself or just accept that she sometimes doesn't follow through when I would like her too. I might believe that she should call, but the facts are that she rarely does."

At this point, Emily can choose to accept the situation or may want to assertively ask her mom to be more responsive. We will address assertiveness later.

Name Calling

A third form of thinking that happens particularly with people is name calling. When you use name calling, you are using some name or term to sum somebody up, rather than describing the situation. In Bob's case, if something goes wrong, he might call himself a "failure" rather than say, "This is not how I intended it to turn out." Bob might call someone who compliments him "insincere" or even "a liar," following up on the thought that they were just saying something to be nice.

The problem with name calling is that it paints ourselves and others with too broad a brush. We have all failed at times, but it is not helpful to call ourselves or others failures because we have all succeeded as well. We all lie, and we all tell the truth. While name calling may be intended to be helpful, it often serves more as an impediment.

Removing the Names

Again, mindfulness can be particularly helpful in moving from name calling to a more useful way of responding to people and yourself. A name takes a specific situation and generalizes it to encompass everything about someone (she is an *uncaring failure* of a mother). Using mindful techniques, you describe the situation to yourself as clearly as you can, without judging the behavior or generalizing beyond the immediate situation. Instead of saying,

"She's a bad mother," Emily can simply describe the actual situation, "She has not called me since we last spoke."

Name calling is similar to all-or-nothing thinking and can similarly be challenged. Like all-or-nothing thoughts, you can ask yourself if there is any evidence that the name is not completely true: "Well, she is not a completely bad mother. She tells me she loves me, and she is very encouraging. Just because she doesn't call when I want her to doesn't cancel out the positives."

Activities and People

In addressing thinking about people, we generally focused on decreasing dysfunctional thoughts about them. Here we will focus on increasing fun and rewarding activities with people. As mentioned in the beginning of this chapter, being with other people can either be a source of enjoyment or of pain. When we are depressed, we tend to anticipate increased pain, so we stop doing things. To fix this, you can set up a plan to increase the fun things you can do with someone else.

There are three reasons to increase activities with others. First, many things are more enjoyable with other people. Second, if you commit to doing something with someone else, it may increase the likelihood that you will follow through. Third, by spending time with someone, you may develop a better friendship, and that relationship may become even more supportive.

The following exercise is meant to help you to schedule an activity with someone. At the very least, it will help you have a pleasant activity. It may also help you start increasing your rewarding contacts with people.

1. Make a weekly activity schedule for the upcoming week, like the one that you filled out in chapter 5. Record all the things you currently have planned.

2. Make a list of times that you could schedule an activity for at least an hour. Choose at least three times so you have some options.

3. Review your list of pleasant activities. Choose three activities that can be done with someone else.

4. Identify people with whom you could do pleasant activities (do not evaluate whether they are a good choice or not— just write down everyone who pops in your head).

5. Choose an easy activity and someone to do it with

6. Call up the person and ask. If they aren't there, leave a message proposing the activity, along with the time and date.

Now, this is a pretty easy list to write, but each step can be a chance to get stuck. Here are some roadblocks that can get in the way, and some solutions.

Roadblock	Solution
Thoughts: I don't have time. It won't work. They'll say no. I'll look like an idiot.	Use a thought record to evaluate the thoughts.
Feelings: Too tired, unmotivated, depressed, embarrassed, or shy.	1. Remind yourself that you don't have to feel like doing something to do it. 2. Do a mindfulness exercise to notice your internal state and how it is influencing your actions.
Activities: Watching TV, sleeping, "frittering."	Set a specific time for your task. If necessary, unplug your TV (you can always plug it in once you are doing healthier things).
Organization: Not having a clear activity planned, details worked out, or a backup if the first plan doesn't work out.	1. Use a calendar to schedule. 2. Have a friend remind you.
Other people: Demands, requests, criticisms, or judgements.	1. Practice saying "no" to requests (see next chapter). 2. Schedule the needs of others around your planned activity.

The overall point is don't let anything stop you from trying! There is always a way to move forward towards a better mood!

Who To Do Things With

It's probably easier to start practicing these skills with someone with whom you have an established, social relationship. Later you can practice in establishing new relationships.

If you are not in a dating relationship, it probably makes sense not to practice both doing new activities *and* initiating a dating or a romantic relationship at the same time. Either do new activities with an old friend or old activities with a new friend. If you are currently married, dating, or involved in a romantic relationship, this may be a very good person to invite to share new activities with you.

Start with easy things for you and for the other person. Be open to hearing "no." If a person does turn you down, use your thought-challenging skills to examine what you tell yourself about that response.

Summary

The skills you have been learning can be very rewarding when you apply them to dealing with people. By practicing the thoughts and activity skills with people, you will improve your skills and increase positive interactions with those around you. Take advantage of the possibilities for joy that being with other people holds. It may be difficult at first, but with practice and the skills you've learned in this book so far, you will become more available to the pleasures of company.

8

people skills

How to Make Talking Helpful

Depression is often associated with two relationship problems: the lack of supportive, helpful contacts with people and the presence of unhealthy interactions. You might find that as you get depressed you don't feel like hanging out with friends and you avoid people. Alternatively, you may find that people who didn't previously bother you now really get on your nerves. You might be more irritable and get into arguments more often, or you might not say what you're thinking at all. You could become passive and let other people make decisions for you.

In thinking about how people might play a role in your depression, you can consider the core belief that you identified. You might notice that some of the examples (like, "I'm worthless unless I am loved") are specifically about your interactions with others. However, even beliefs that aren't clearly related to people (like, "I must succeed to feel good about myself") often have an interpersonal component (who is evaluating your success?). As with other things, how your interactions with people affect your mood will depend on how you think about them. In addition, you can learn to act in ways that increases the chance that your interactions are positive for you and those in your life.

In this chapter, we will review four specific skills for dealing with people: listening, expressing yourself, making requests, and saying yes or no. These may sound very simple. However, most people find some of these skills difficult in some situations, and people who are depressed often have difficulty with one or more of these skills.

We encourage you to try out the activities and skills presented in this chapter. One word of preparation, however. Oftentimes making requests and responding to requests are the hardest skills to learn. As with learning any new behavior, it is helpful to start with easier situations and to work up to those that are more difficult. Using your mindfulness exercises can be a very important tool to help you practice learning new ways of interacting with people.

Listening

You might be surprised that we start with listening to other people when discussing people skills. However, learning to listen has several important benefits. Listening is less threatening to do than asking for stuff. It stops you from spending too much time in your own head. It helps you to stop mindreading and have a more accurate understanding of what the person you are with is really saying. In addition, when you listen well the other person probably enjoys the conversation more and this may lead to a better conversation for both of you.

What do we mean by listening? You might think that listening is paying attention and trying to understand what is said. However, we define listening in a more active way. In our sense, listening is also providing feedback to the speaker so they get a sense of what you heard. Listening skills really are "responding" skills; that is, ways of letting the person you are talking to know that you're paying attention. By taking the time to let the person you're talking to know what you heard, you also force yourself to pay more attention and may actually hear them better!

Body Language

The simplest ways to let someone know you are listening is to use body language. You will probably recognize the things on the list below that show you are listening:

✦ *Good eye-contact:* Looking at the speaker's face

✦ *Facial expression:* Matching the topic being discussed (smile when talking about jokes; frowning when hearing about an injustice)

✦ *Relaxed but attentive posture:* Not slouching, not so rigid that you appear tense

Mindfulness is a very useful skill in developing awareness of your body language. By practicing the observational and mindfulness skills we've been working on while engaged in conversation, you have a chance to improve those skills while simultaneously noting important aspects of how you communicate. You then have the choice to continue behaving as you do or to make a change.

Check Out Your Body

In your next conversation, do a "mini" mindful body scan. Notice your level of eye contact, facial expression, and posture (the position of your body). Remember not to judge—just notice. Notice how these three things change in relation to your mood, the topic, or the mood and style of the other person.

Voice Quality

As important as what you say can be how you say it. Pay attention to:

✦ *Loudness:* Speak up so that the other person can hear you, but don't yell.

✦ *Speak clearly:* Pay attention to pronunciation. Mumbling makes it harder for others to hear you.

✦ *Rate of speech:* Notice how fast or slowly you talk. Take the time to think before talking.

Check Your Voice

In your next conversation, do another mini mindful body scan. Notice your voice quality: loudness, pronunciation, and rate of speech. As always, remember not to judge—just notice. Notice how these three things change in relation to your mood, the topic, or the mood and style of the other person.

Let Them Know You're Listening

While body language and voice quality can be great indications that you're paying attention, they are not sufficient for assuring your speaker that you really understand. To do that, you need to give them some feedback. Here are some ways to do that.

Verbal Prompts

Verbal prompts are the normal, everyday cues we use to say that we're paying attention, like "yeah," "uh-huh," and so forth. Even things like, "I hear you," or, "I know what you mean," fall in this category.

The good thing about a verbal prompt is that it lets the person know that you are aware that they are talking. However, it doesn't let the person know what you're hearing from them. When you say "I know what you mean," neither you or the person speaking really find out if you know what they mean. That requires you to give the person more information. The next examples tell you how to do that.

Paraphrasing

Paraphrasing simply means telling the person what you heard them say in your own words. Consider how Bob lets his wife, Sandra, know that he's heard her.

Sandra: I really need you to pick up the kids today. I'm completely overwhelmed and need a break.

Bob: *(paraphrasing his wife)* You'd like me to pick up the kids to take some of the pressure off you.

In this example, Bob just basically tells his wife what he's heard. This is pretty simple, but it can be very powerful. Consider some of the other things he could have said:

+ *"Sorry, I don't have time."* This ignores the major concern, that his wife is feeling overwhelmed.

+ *"Okay."* This is more helpful, but it doesn't give any evidence that Bob is really noticing what is going on with his wife.

+ *"Well, I'm at the end of my rope, too."* This minimizes his wife's concerns and puts the two of them in competition to prove who is more stressed (no winners here!).

One thing that also is important to note: just as acceptance is not surrender, listening is not agreeing. When you listen, you acknowledge the other person's message—but that does not mean you agree with it. By paraphrasing, Bob did not say he would or wouldn't help out. However, because he's shown that he's listening, his wife is probably more receptive to either answer. Some people resist using listening skills because they worry that acknowledging someone's opinion means that you agree. You might want to notice if thoughts like this come up for you, and if so, test the thought by experimenting with listening skills.

As you might have noted, this kind of paraphrasing helps Bob pay attention to what his wife is concerned about. However, his wife was pretty specific about what was going on. Sometimes people are more vague. The following skill can help both in listening and helping to clarify what has been said.

Reflection

Reflection is a skill that, like paraphrasing, lets the listener know what you heard them say. However, in addition, in reflection you "reflect" the emotion or underlying message that you are hearing as well. Let's see how Bob does this with Sandra.

Sandra: *(in an irritable tone)* I really need you to pick up the kids today.

Bob: I get the impression that you're pretty stressed today. You'd like me to help out by getting the kids.

In this case, Bob is reflecting the emotional side of the message that he hears (that Sandra is stressed). The biggest challenge we hear from people trying to learn to reflect is the fear that they will get the feeling wrong. We even hear this from new therapists learning to do psychotherapy. The important thing here is to remember that whether you are right or wrong in your reflection, trying is likely going to improve communication either way. In the example above, Bob might or might not be right. However, that is less important than trying. If he's not on the money, his wife can clarify for him how she feels. Whether he is right or not, she knows that he's trying to pay attention and understand where she's coming from.

Paraphrasing and reflection overlap. The main point of both of these skills is to pay attention to:

1. What is being asked or said.

2. What emotion or desire is behind the message.

Now It's Your Turn

For the next week, practice paraphrasing and reflection. For the first three days, practice paraphrasing. For the last four, practice both paraphrasing and reflection. To practice, simply paraphrase or reflect *every* statement someone else makes to you before you tell them what is on your mind. If you are anxious about this, you can set up an exposure hierarchy. Start with a person who you feel will be supportive. It could even be a friend who knows what you are trying to learn. Practice paraphrasing and reflecting with this person for a week, then move on to other people on your hierarchy who would be more challenging.

Expressing Yourself

Listening does not require you to express your own opinions, feelings, experiences, and so on. Expressing yourself requires additional skills. Now, it may seem surprising, but expressing yourself clearly is often very hard to do and can be particularly hard to do when you're depressed.

What makes it so hard? Probably your core beliefs. For example, if Bob believes he isn't good enough, he then probably feels that his opinions don't matter as much as other people's because he matters less as a person than they do. He probably also assumes that others see him as he sees himself and don't think he deserves to ask for things. This might lead him to focus only on what others want and not express his needs.

On the other hand, someone with a belief like, "The world is unfair and overwhelming," may feel angry and anxious as well as depressed. This person may feel that their needs aren't recognized and may consequently express them in an aggressive and angry manner. While this is completely understandable given their experience of the world, it may not work very well.

These two examples highlight two general styles of responding. The first is passive (not expressing yourself, or expressing yourself in an indirect or unclear way) and the second is aggressive (expressing your needs in a way that attacks the listener). While both of these styles are at times useful, for most situations a middle ground is usually more effective.

That middle ground is what is called *assertive communication.* A lot of people have written about assertiveness, and you likely have your own understanding of what assertiveness is. However, just to make sure we're all on the same page, here's what we mean by assertiveness: Assertiveness is speaking in a way that clearly communicates what you want to say but that also respects the rights and needs of those around you, particularly the listener.

In contrast to assertiveness, when you use passive communication you are not being clear about your needs but are focused more on the needs or desires of your listener. Aggressive communication occurs when you ask or say something and don't acknowledge that the listener's point of view matters.

Here's an example to clarify passive and aggressive communication. Remember that Bob held the core belief, "I'm not good enough." How did this play out in his relationships? Bob always assumed that if something was wrong or someone was angry, it was because he had done something wrong. He never criticized others, but leaped to the assumption, "I screwed up." He never expressed his preferences because he thought he might be unreasonable. When people would choose to do things he did not want to do, he would be resentful, but also feel guilty ("I don't deserve to feel this way").

Bob's behavior was generally an example of a passive communication style. Bob was not always passive, however. As he became depressed, he also became more irritable. He found himself criticizing others in his mind as selfish and uncaring because they didn't notice how much he was suffering and "never" paid attention to his needs. Remember, Bob often used passive communication, and sometimes he felt like he did express his needs. However, because he was so indirect, other people often didn't notice and Bob ended up feeling ignored.

One day Bob's wife asked him to pick up the kids (ages six and eight) on his way home from work. Although Bob would have to cancel an afternoon meeting, he agreed without telling his wife about this conflict (passive communication). He ended up feeling irritable, thinking, "She should know that this really would disrupt my work!" On the way home, the children were arguing in the car. Bob stopped the car and yelled at both of the children, telling them they were "ungrateful brats." This situation is a clear example of aggressive communication (he attacked the kids verbally, meeting his need of venting his anger but ignoring that they both might have had problems that needed to be addressed).

In general, assertive behavior tends to be more effective than passive or aggressive communication. However, you might be thinking about examples where this is not the case. We often hear people in treatment say, "If I'm being robbed, I am not going to be assertive!" We want to encourage you not to throw the baby out with the bathwater. There are times when aggressive or passive behavior may be necessary or more effective than assertive communication. However, these are more often the exceptions than the rule. We encourage you to try out being assertive in more areas of your life and consider this an experiment to see if this new behavior helps improve your mood.

In the next sections we review three skills that aide effective, assertive communication.

"I" Statements

The first step in assertive communication is to be direct, and the easiest way to do this is through "I" statements. These are exactly what they sound like. You state what you're thinking or feeling, generally starting the sentence with "I," such as, "I feel sad," "I want to go to the beach," or, "I really need your help." I statements are used to focus on our own feelings and actions rather than others. By talking from your own perspective, it reduces the amount you put the other person on the defensive or make them feel attacked. In addition, it reduces the assumptions involved; you are talking about your own feelings, thoughts, and actions, rather than those of somebody else. You can better observe your own experiences.

We think of I statements as just describing your state. Mindfulness practice can improve your ability to use I statements, by helping to observe your state—including your emotions, thoughts, and desires—and describe them accurately.

Simple, right? However, you might notice some thoughts that interfere with using I statements. One thought that often comes out of a core belief of, "I'm undeserving," is, "I'm being selfish." Many people feel that I statements come off as impolite or too forward. Some people have a belief that, "I shouldn't ask for anything." These thoughts and beliefs can make it very hard to use I statements.

If you are questioning whether it is reasonable to use I statements, use the two techniques from the thought-challenging section. First, check the thinking errors and challenge them. Second, test out your thoughts. Try I statements and see how you feel and how other people react.

Clarifying

Clarifying is just being very specific about something. Instead of saying something general and global like, "You never do anything," a clear statement is easily defined. The primary components of a clarifying statement are:

✦ Specifying the situation ("When _____ happens"), then

✦ Stating your experience ("I feel/want/need/ _____ .")

For example, "I get tired and irritable when I have to pick up the kids and then make dinner," is a good clear statement because it is specific about what the situation is and how it makes the person feel. I statements help with clarifying because they make it clear that whatever is being expressed is your personal opinion or feeling.

The clearer and more specific your statement, the more likely you are to be understood. Here are several points to help:

✦ To make a statement clear, use specific terms ("I need you to pick up the kids") instead of generalizations ("I need some help"). The more specific, the more likely the person will know what you want and whether or not they can do it.

✦ If you think back to the thoughts chapter (chapter 5), the techniques for challenging unhelpful thoughts can help you in also making clearer statements. Notice whether you are thinking in generalizations, all-or-nothings, or shoulds, and try to rephrase these experiences in terms of your own reactions and specific preferences.

Making Requests

Many of our interactions with people revolve around requests. Making clear, positive requests is a critical part of assertiveness. If you don't let others know what you need in a way they can understand, it is unlikely they can help you.

To make an assertive request, you combine an I statement with a clarifying comment, and then specify what you would like. For example: "I get overwhelmed when I think about picking up the kids and then having to make dinner, and I would like you to pick up the kids tonight." This statement lets the listener know how the speaker is feeling, clarifies the situation, and tells the listener specifically what the speaker would like. Let's compare it to some other statements.

✦ "I want you to pick up the kids," doesn't tell the listener why this is important.

✦ "I'm overwhelmed," doesn't provide any solutions or guidance to the listener about how to help.

✦ "You should pick up the kids," doesn't respect the fact that the listener may have competing needs.

There are several things that can improve your assertive requests. First, try to stick with facts and evidence when making a request, rather than resorting to assuming and mindreading. Oftentimes depression can lead you to misinterpret the intentions of those around you. For example, you might think someone isn't doing what you would like because they don't care, when in fact they may not know what you want. Rather than attacking them for being uncaring or not speaking because you "know" it won't help, just tell the person, and consider it an experiment to test out your beliefs.

Second, if possible ask the listener to do something rather than to not do something ("Please listen," rather than, "Stop yelling," for example). It's easier for people to replace an old behavior with a new behavior than it is to stop an old behavior and have no new options.

Third, be a "broken record." If the listener changes the topic, use a listening statement, either a paraphrase or a reflection, then politely restate the request. Do this until the listener responds to your request.

Fourth, practice this with easier situations first. Try to be assertive with a friend, or try making positive requests (for example, "I really had a great time the last time we got together, and I would like to do it again. Can I treat you to lunch?"). You can practice the skills with positive situations like giving compliments or acknowledging kindnesses before moving on to more confrontive or challenging conversations.

Fifth, as you make requests, do so mindfully. Notice the thoughts, physical sensations, and emotions that occur before, during, and after you have tried to make an assertive comment. Interactions with people can be very provocative internally, even if they appear completely benign to the outside world. You may find that your internal reactions when trying to be assertive tell you a lot about yourself and your core beliefs.

Finally, hear the response. Practice listening to make sure you understand what the response is. It may not be what you want, but if you were assertive, it may at least clarify the situation. Oftentimes, stating your needs clears a lot of stuff up and things get better. Sometimes, stating what you need leads to the awareness that what you want is not available from that person. While this may be disappointing, at least you know where you stand, and you can move forward from that point. Alternatively, a response might tell you that you weren't actually as assertive as might be necessary in this situation. You can then try and problem solve how to improve your request.

If you are anxious doing these things, you can play out your request ahead of time. Actually say out loud what you want to ask and then say the response you think you are likely to get, as well as any responses you really fear you might get. When you hear the responses, ask yourself how you would feel about them and how you would respond. Observe how your feelings relate to the response and how the responses relate to your core beliefs.

Here is an example. Bob was a partner in a small company with his brother Mike. Mike was responsible for finances, while Bob was responsible for operating the company. He was frustrated enough with how his brother managed the budget that Bob was going to leave the business. Prior to that, he decided to try using his assertiveness skills. He practiced for a few days and imagined a variety of outcomes, including agreeing to end the business. When he actually approached his brother, he made the following request: "Mike, I need to talk to you. I am very worried about the accounts. When you pay all the bills at the first of the month, it leaves me no funds for unexpected expenses. I need us to come to an agreement so I have at least two thousand dollars available for potential emergencies each month."

Bob used I statements ("I need to talk to you," "I am worried"), clarified the situation (how the bills are paid and the lack of an emergency account) and made a specific request (keep two thousand dollars as a backup fund). As it turned out, Mike had not realized that Bob was stressed about having a safety net, and thought that paying out money as it came in would make him feel better. Mike agreed to set up an emergency fund; they negotiated the amount and how soon it would be set up.

Make Your Requests

Now it's your turn to make some requests. Here are some reminders to help you:

+ Identify three requests that you would like to make. Rank them from easiest to hardest.

+ Write out the easiest request in the following model: Your I statement, clarifying the situation, then making a specific, positive request.

+ Choose a time and a place and make the request.

+ Before, during, and after the request, do a mini body scan and notice your thoughts, feelings, and physical sensations.

+ Examine how close to your written model your assertiveness was. Do not evaluate your effectiveness based on what the response was, but on how close your actual message was to your intended message.

+ Practice the next request.

How to Say Yes or No

You've learned about making requests, now you get to read about the other side: saying yes or no to requests. In some ways, this section is simpler, but the actual practice can be harder. Responding to requests provides many opportunities for our core beliefs to play out. You might think you don't deserve to say yes to some requests (asked out on a date) or no to others (asked to help someone move). You might feel incompetent and refuse because you expect to fail, or you might respond based on a sense of frustration and a feeling that the request is unjust because you see the world as unjust.

One of the difficulties with responding to requests is that you may not feel that you have adequate time to prepare for them. They usually occur on someone else's timetable. This might make it hard to remember to use your communication skills and to be mindful of your experience in the moment. However, there are some simple steps that can improve your ability to respond to requests in a way that is assertive, respecting both yourself and the speaker.

Saying Yes

In theory, saying yes to a request you would like to fulfill is easy. Just say it. It can be helpful to add a comment about what you see as positive about the request ("I appreciate that you thought of me. Sure, I'll go").

Saying yes to positive requests can be a problem if you are depressed and unmotivated or fearful. In this case, it can be helpful to say yes, but do so in a way that helps you address your concerns. To do so:

+ State the positive about the request ("I really appreciate that you thought of me").

+ Acknowledge your concern ("But I'm pretty worn out, and I may have a hard time keeping up with you").

+ Say yes, giving the other person a chance to respond to your concern ("I'm happy to go, if you are okay with us taking a slow pace").

In this approach, you basically put things on the table. The speaker has the choice to follow through or not, depending on whether your proposed modification of the request is acceptable. In doing so, remember to notice any thoughts that might undermine your agreeing to something you might enjoy. These can include mindreading ("He's just asking 'cause he feels sorry for me"), shoulds and predicting the future ("I shouldn't go—I'll drag everyone down"), and labeling ("I'm such a fraud; I shouldn't go because I'll just be pretending to enjoy myself"). Notice these thoughts, recognize them as just thoughts, and remember that they do not have to guide your decision.

Saying No

Saying no is not all that different from saying yes. The steps are:

+ State the positive about the request ("I really appreciate that you thought of me").

+ Say no ("But thrash metal is not my style, so I'll take a pass").

+ Give the other person an alternative ("How about if we get together for a blues concert?").

A critical point about saying no is being succinct and to the point. If you beat around the bush, you might end up saying yes or leaving the other person with the impression that you said yes. This can lead to confusion and conflict. You also don't need to justify your decision (in the example above, you could just say, "No thanks," rather than explaining your musical tastes). The decision is yours to make.

Saying no (or yes, for that matter) can be harder in situations where there is a power differential (like with a boss or with parents) or where you are very concerned about maintaining a good relationship (say, with a spouse or partner or with extended family). Again, being mindful in situations where you say no, or where you would like to say no but don't, can help you learn more about your core beliefs and then start choosing whether to listen to them.

Say Yes or No

Experiment with responding to requests, remembering these key tips:

+ Mindfully observe yourself responding to requests for the next three days or until you receive at least one request.

+ Following the request, practice saying yes or no as described above, and mindfully notice your own reaction and that of the requestor.

Not Easy, but Worth It

Practicing the communications skills of listening, assertiveness, requests, and saying yes or no can have several benefits. You might find that your interactions improve. You may also observe more about your core beliefs and develop a better understanding of how they influence your interactions. Finally, you may find that some of your fears regarding how people will respond to you are inaccurate or at least exaggerated. These skills are some of the most challenging to learn, but as with many challenges, the payoff can be great!

9

depression and exercise

Depression is generally thought to be an illness of the mind, but when you look at the toll that it takes on the body, it becomes clear that depression is an illness of the body, not just the mind. Exercise engages both your mind and body in the fight to overcome depression and thus can be one of your most powerful tools in bringing you out of depression.

This chapter will discuss how to consciously use your body to decrease depression and enhance living mindfully. We will look at the research on exercise and depression and what it tells us about why exercise helps in depression. We will also discuss how exercise affects sleep and how you can use exercise to get a better night's sleep, an important factor in helping you feel better. And finally, using the principles of cognitive behavioral therapy and mindfulness, we will consider how you can implement an exercise plan.

Living in Your Body

While you live in your body day and night, year after year, it can sometimes come as a surprise to realize that, indeed, you are your body! Indeed, how you perceive and experience your body has a deep connection to your sense of well-being. The great benefit of using exercise to alleviate depression is that first of all, it is highly effective, and secondly, it gives you a new relationship with your body. When you combine the observational skills of CBT and mindfulness, you gain a whole new capacity to become intimate with yourself as you develop an exercise routine for the alleviation of depression. Mindfulness helps you tune in to the subtle changes that occur when you exercise. The observational tools of CBT and mindfulness help you watch the mind and see the thoughts about exercise, be they positive or negative thoughts, and realize that they are merely thoughts, not necessarily facts. You can use your newly developed skills of paying attention moment by moment to the sensations in your body as you exercise and perhaps experience a new relationship with your body. The many evaluation skills learned through CBT can be applied to evaluating the effectiveness of exercise. We will explore how you can use your skills of mindfulness and CBT to enhance your attunement to your body.

The Body Blahs

The ways in which depression affects the body (depression's somatic symptoms) are often the motivating factors for people to seek treatment for depression. Depressed folks are most often treated in primary care clinics (Katon 1992) rather than mental-health clinics, in part because they are not sleeping well, they have less energy, they are tired, they have more aches, pains, and physical worries, and they are either eating too much or have no appetite. As you know, these are some of the common symptoms of depression that directly impact the physical body, or what we call the "body blahs." For many people, and particularly in some cultures, these symptoms are all that people acknowledge as their depressive symptoms. Regardless if people are able to acknowledge that they are depressed, their body knows the blahs have taken over.

What does the physical nature of depression suggest about treatment? Many clients tell us, "I feel so bad, I can't do anything," and the idea of exercising seems crazy. When we look at the evidence, however, we usually find that when people get active they feel better. Conversely, when people go with the feelings of low energy and exhaustion and stop doing things, they get caught in a downward spiral and feel even worse. Therefore, paying attention to your body and getting active can be a critical part of recovering from depression.

Exercise and Depression: What the Research Shows

The research on exercise and depression shows that exercise has both psychological and physical benefits (Byrne 1993). Almost everybody is familiar with the sense of mastery that comes from keeping to an exercise routine. When you exercise regularly there is the sense that you are in control and capable of taking care of yourself. When you are depressed, you often feel out of control and unable to do anything that will help you feel better. If you are depressed, you're familiar with the downward spiral of not doing anything, which leads you to feel less energetic, which then makes it harder to get motivated to do activities. Naturally, under these conditions, your self-esteem can take a nosedive. This effect isn't surprising to those of us who are familiar with the research, as fifty-one studies found a positive link between exercise and an increase in self-esteem (Spence 1997).

Aside from the increase in self-esteem, there is just the sheer release of pent up tension that occurs with movement of the body. You have probably had the experience of feeling a drop in frustration, anxiety, or even anger after exercise. The change in physical tension alone can be a powerful motivator or reinforcement for getting out and moving.

Exercise directly alters brain chemistry. Cortisol is a hormone that is elevated with stress, anxiety, and depression. When you are stressed your adrenal glands pump out high levels of this stress hormone, which in turns flips the switch telling the body it's time to increase the heart rate, and blood pressure and get ready for new threats. Exercise reduces cortisol levels in the brain, thus helping the body to relax rather than prepare for battle. Particularly if you have a depression that also includes a high degree of anxiety, exercise may be especially helpful because of the cortisol-reducing benefits (Gorman 2002).

The release of endorphins, the body's own pain-relieving and mood-elevating chemicals, is a commonly acclaimed benefit of exercise. Endorphins are often linked to a "runner's high," a greatly increased sense of well-being. Exercise consistently triggers a release of endorphins, but the research is still out on whether exercise produces enough endorphins to decrease depression alone (Casper 1993). There is no doubt, however, that active exercise does increase endorphins.

Exercise is associated with the same chemical benefits as antidepressant medications: it increases the availability of the neurotransmitters, such as serotonin, in the brain (Dunn 1991). The well-known group of antidepressant medications called serotonin-reuptake inhibitors (SSRIs) is famous for increasing the availability of the neurotransmitter serotonin at the receptor sites in the brain. However, with exercise you get the benefits without the side effects common with antidepressant medications. In particular 10 percent to 40 percent of patients who take SSRIs (Celexa, Lexapro, Luvox, Paxil, Prozac, and Zoloft) will experience some sexual dysfunctions such as lack of sexual drive, difficulty reaching orgasm, or difficulty maintaining an erection in males (Stahl 2000).

Let's look at some of the studies that have examined the link between exercise and depression. In one study (Doyne 1987), forty depressed women were randomly assigned to eight weeks of running, a weight-lifting program, or a wait list (the control group). The women who were assigned to running or weightlifting were less depressed then the control group at the end of the trial and at one-, seven-, and twelve-month follow-ups. Of interest in this study was that the women's cardiovascular fitness did not improve significantly, whereas their mood did.

A study of a group of people who were depressed enough that they needed to be hospitalized found significant reduction in depression among patients who were prescribed an aerobic exercise program, but not in the control group who participated in occupational therapy (doing crafts and talking) but didn't exercise (Matinsen 1985).

Another study looked at older adults who had not responded well to antidepressant therapy. These patients were randomly placed into either exercise classes or health education talks for ten weeks, 55 percent of the exercise group versus 33 percent of the health education talks experienced a greater than 30 percent decline in depression. The implication of the study is that adding exercise to usual antidepressant therapy is very promising, particularly for those people who are not responding to medications alone (Mather 2002).

The prevention of relapse is a major concern among depression researchers. In 1999, Duke University researcher James Blumenthal, Ph.D. divided 150 depressed subjects aged fifty or more into three groups: one was put on an exercise regimen, another was given the medication Zoloft (an SSRI), and the third was given a combination of the two (1999). The folks who were in the exercise group worked out three times a week for thirty minutes on a treadmill or stationary bicycle at 70 to 85 percent of their maximum heart rate. While all three groups showed significantly lower rates of depression after four months, the pleasant surprise was that six months later the exercise group experienced significantly less relapse than those in the Zoloft or combination groups. Only 8 percent of the exercise group had their depression return compared to 38 percent of the Zoloft group and 31 percent of the combined medication/exercise group. Blumenthal speculated that the group of patients who exercised may have felt a sense of accomplishment, which could have made them feel more self-confident and have better self esteem, whereas the group who were taking the pills were not as active in fighting depression. The researchers further speculated whether some of the benefits to the exercise group were due to the support obtained from working out together.

Exercise: What Type and How Long?

It's natural to wonder what type of exercise you should be doing to get relief from depression. What the research generally states about this question is that you should do exercise that you enjoy and that you want to do. Most research is based on aerobic exercise, but certainly a wide variety of exercise has been found to reduce depression, including yoga, tai chi, and weight lifting. What's most important is that you choose something that you are motivated to do and that will be easy to sustain.

Many of the studies have people exercising three times a week, for thirty minutes each time, as a baseline for determining whether exercise helps with depression. This is a useful baseline to use as you develop your exercise program. Improvements in your mood and relief from anxiety are consistently associated with keeping with an exercise program for ten weeks or more. This is not to say that you are going to have to wait for ten weeks to feel better, as you will likely feel some of the psychological boost of improved self-esteem along with improved energy from the onset of exercise (Artal 1998).

The good news is that you don't have to be fit to get the mood benefits from exercise. If you are out of shape, overweight, and deeply familiar with the couch potato position, you are a prime candidate to benefit from moderate exercise. Of course, if you have a heart condition, or major medical complications, you should seek the advice of your doctor before launching an exercise regimen.

Often a structured program is a big help in getting motivated and sticking with exercise. If you have made a commitment to a class or walking with a friend, it is much more difficult to wiggle out of it than if you just tell yourself that you'll go for a walk when it's convenient. Most of us have an inexhaustible fund of seemingly logical reasons not to exercise; thus, when you make a commitment to exercise with others you can bypass your personal storehouse of excuses.

Sleep and Exercise

Sleep disturbance can be a key problem for the person struggling with depression. Sleeping problems are often the complaints that initially bring people suffering with depression to the doctor. Sleep can also be disturbed because of side effects from prescribed medications, medical causes, or because you have a sleep disorder; however, depression and anxiety are the lead psychiatric causes of insomnia. With depression, the architecture of sleep gets disturbed at the front, middle, and end of a night's sleep: a depressed person cannot fall asleep, is wide awake in the middle of the night, or is awake in the early morning, despite being very tired. Sometimes depression also causes hypersomnia, when people sleep beyond what is normal for them.

People who exercise regularly have fewer problems with sleep-lessness. Exercise enhances your sleep quality by promoting a smoother and more regular transition between the cycles and phases of sleep. Exercise improves sleep because it is a physical stressor to the body. The brain compensates for the physical stress by increasing deep sleep. Moderate exercise lasting twenty to thirty minutes three to four times a week will help you increase stage-four sleep, your deepest sleep cycle. A controlled study of thirty-two older adults (ages sixty to eighty-four) who had major depression or dysthymia found that a ten-week program of weight training exercise (three times a week) significantly improved all self-rated sleep and depression measures (Singh 1997).

Shining Light on the Matter

There is an interesting relationship between sunlight, sleep, and exercise. Exposure to sunlight influences your circadian rhythms, which are the biological rhythms of your body that fluctuate around every twenty-four hours. As explained in *All I Want Is a Good Night's Sleep*, our "circadian rhythms interact with each other; for example core body temperature interacts with the sleep-wake cycle. We become sleepy whenever our body temperature begins to drop (in the afternoon after it hits its zenith) and again in the evening. This explains why we often feel more tired in the afternoon and again at night" (1996, 69). Exercise improves sleep by producing a significant rise in body temperature followed by a compensatory drop a few hours later. The drop in body temperature, which occurs two to four hours after exercise, makes it easier to fall asleep and stay asleep. Therefore you may want to avoid exercising just before you go to bed. Researchers have traditionally suggested that you should plan your exercise for the afternoon if you are having trouble falling asleep at night. However, this notion is under question in the sleep literature, and what would be best is if you experiment with the timing of your exercise, and even consider late night exercise if that is the window of exercise opportunity that exists for you (Youngstedt 2000).

Inadequate exposure to bright light is associated with seasonal affective disorder (when you get depressed in the winter because the days are short), as well as disturbed sleep. Combining exercise with the great outdoors provides the treatment advantage of exposure to sunlight. If you're having trouble sleeping it's possible your circadian rhythms are disturbed. Exercising outside with exposure to the sunlight could help regulate your sleep cycle. Generally speaking, if you are having trouble falling asleep at night and cannot pull yourself out of bed in the morning you need to get exposure to light in the early morning hours. It would be best for you to pull yourself out of bed and go for a walk when the roosters are crowing. This will help you regulate your sleep back to the normal hours of falling asleep around 10 P.M. to 11 P.M. and waking up at 6 A.M. to 7 A.M. If you are on the other end of the spectrum and falling asleep in the late afternoon or early evening (which is common for the elderly), and sleeping until the middle of the night, you would benefit from exposure to light in the late afternoon. That is when you need to take your walk.

Exercise Advantage

There are many health benefits to developing an exercise program whether or not you are depressed. Aerobic exercise increases the pumping capacities of the heart and decreases the buildup of plaque in the arteries. Regular exercise reduces the risk for high blood pressure. And if you already have high blood pressure, moderate exercise can help lower it (Blair 1984). Exercise can also modify cholesterol levels. Physical activity reduces low-density lipoprotein (LDL), which is good because this type of cholesterol forms plaques in the arteries. At the same time, exercise increases high-density lipoprotein (HDL), which clears up deposits of cholesterol in arteries, thus reducing the risk for heart disease (Pronk 1997).

Everybody knows that exercise helps with weight management, and any tour of a self-help aisle in a bookstore will show you dozens of ways to combine exercise with dieting to reach your goal weight. What is less commonly known is that regular exercise has been shown to reduce the risk for certain types of cancer. For example, one study concluded that moderately active men had half the colon cancer risk compared to men who were inactive (Lee 1991). Exercise is tremendously helpful in the management of diabetes, an illness that is causing more and more problems as the general populations becomes increasingly obese. Weight bearing exercise is documented to prevent osteoporosis and helps with the treatment of this problem. Chronic low back pain is also helped with regular exercise.

It doesn't take a rocket scientist to see that there are many reasons to move the body on a regular basis. The benefits are broad, profound, and engaging. The advantages of developing an exercise routine are crystal clear. And yet depression is an illness that robs one of energy, motivation, and interest. Thus, putting an exercise routine into place can be a monumental hurdle for the depressed individual. The tools of CBT and mindfulness can help you overcome this hurdle towards managing your depression as well as realizing a new level of fitness.

Using CBT and Mindfulness: The Why, What, and When

Before you start an exercise program it is helpful to look at yourself with sweet curiosity and tough honesty, two states of mind that CBT and mindfulness share. You can ask yourself simply: Why do I want to exercise? What do I want to do for exercise? When can I exercise? Pragmatically, you may also want to flip the questions and consider what would keep your exercise plan from working: Why would I stop exercising? What exercise plan would I not keep up? When would I find reasons not to exercise? Don't stop with simple pros and cons of exercising; also consider the pros and cons of not exercising. This will help you understand your basic resistances.

Using the logical part of your mind, you can sit down, divide a paper in half, and explore the answers to these questions. Consider both the short-term and the long-term answers to these questions. What is really difficult to do is to be completely honest with yourself as you consider implementing change. Therefore, we would encourage you to also contemplate these questions using the meditation mind, open to all that passes through, not inhibiting the irrational thoughts as they pass through your awareness.

Let's consider how Emily, our case example from the core beliefs chapter, implemented this strategy. She first examined the pros and cons of why she would want to exercise and the pros and cons of why she would not want to exercise.

PRO: EXERCISING	CON: EXERCISING
I'll feel more energetic.	I'm so tired as it is, I don't know if I have the energy to exercise.
Exercise may help with insomnia.	
Exercise might help me feel less depressed.	I'll probably fail and not stay with it, so I don't want to start.
Exercise is good for my health.	It takes too much time.
I might firm up and lose weight.	I don't like feeling my fat bounce when I exercise.
I would be doing something for myself.	
I feel more alive when I exercise.	I don't like to be seen outside.
	It is going to be uncomfortable.

PRO: NOT EXERCISING	CON: NOT EXERCISING
I don't have to try to change.	I'll probably stay depressed.
I don't have to make any new efforts.	If I stay the same, I'm going to feel like a failure.
I don't have to feel my body; I can stay numb.	
	I'll probably keep feeling embarrassed and uncomfortable about my body.
I don't have to change my schedule.	

From this exercise Emily recognized how uncomfortable she was with her body and how not exercising was a behavioral strategy she used to avoid physically feeling herself. She realized how her core strategy of keeping other people happy helped her avoid paying attention to her own body and her own needs. When she exercised and breathed more deeply she felt more alive but also at times uncomfortable; her usual sense of herself was disturbed by exercise. Her practice of mindfulness meditation helped her see how she had used helping others as a way of not paying attention to herself. She was tired of this pattern and wanted to try breaking it by doing something for herself. When she meditated she noticed how difficult it was for her to just let herself feel her body. She became curious about what it might be like to feel more sensations in her body. She decided to try an exercise program to see if it would help her feel less depressed and more attuned to her body. She used the same pro and con method to sort out what type of exercise she would do. She did this for a few different types of exercise she was interested in pursuing.

PRO: WALKING	CON: WALKING
I can do it easily. I can do it by myself. I can do it before I go to work, at lunch two days a week, or after work. It doesn't cost any money. It is aerobic exercise.	I have to walk outside. If I do it by myself then I can make easy excuses for not doing it. It can be hard to do if the weather is bad.
PRO: NOT WALKING	CON: NOT WALKING
I can sleep in the morning, and eat my lunch leisurely, and get home after work. I don't have to feel uncomfortable exercising outside.	I'll probably stay depressed. I'll continue to avoid feeling myself; I won't change. My health won't improve. I'll continue to have insomnia.

PRO: DOING YOGA	CON: DOING YOGA
I would learn how to stretch my body. This is something I've wanted to do, but have been afraid to try. Yoga can help me develop a new awareness of my body. Yoga would help me learn about my breath. Yoga could help me with my mindfulness meditation practice. Yoga would be a new challenge for me.	It costs money to take classes. I might feel inadequate in classes. I might feel nervous or uncomfortable doing yoga. Yoga is not aerobic exercise. Yoga classes take an hour or more.
PRO: NOT DOING YOGA	**CON: NOT DOING YOGA**
I don't have to feel uncomfortable or nervous. I don't have to pay for a class. I would have time to do something else.	I don't get to learn something new. I'll continue to feel stiff and uncomfortable. I would avoid doing something for myself.

Emily studied her list and decided that she wanted to challenge herself by exercising: she realized she had more to gain than to lose. She decided she would try to exercise three times a week, thinking that if she set the goal to do it every day, she wouldn't follow through and would end up not exercising at all. She decided that since she was uncomfortable about walking outside and being seen by lots of people, she would do her walking in the early morning before people were up and out. She thought about purchasing a treadmill, but decided that would be giving in to her fear of being seen by others. She figured that she could manage to walk before work one day a week and on weekend mornings. Emily also decided to enroll in a beginning yoga class that met once a week in the early evenings. She figured that if she paid for a class that she would likely attend a class, and she thought she would benefit from the support and structure of a yoga class.

Sticking to It

Probably most of us have had the experience of deciding to exercise and then having trouble sticking to this decision. If you are depressed, it's particularly easy to let the apathy associated with depression sink in and control your behavior. To counter this tendency to slip into apathetic lethargy and forget that you ever had an exercise plan, you can devise a Mindfulness Exercise Log. In this log you will want to list your symptoms of depression and then evaluate on a daily basis the strength of these symptoms using a 1 to 10 scale, where 10 represents very strong negative symptoms and 1 represents very light or no negative symptoms. Exercise will typically target your physical symptoms of depression, so this is especially important to track, but you may also want to include some of your cognitive symptoms like concentration, memory, hopelessness, or pessimism to evaluate whether exercise has any impact on these symptoms. Emily's log looked like this.

Emily's Mindfulness Exercise Log

Walk on Monday and Saturday morning
Yoga on Wednesday night
1 = no symptoms: I feel good
10 = intense symptoms: I feel really bad

Symptoms	Mon. W	Tues.	Wed. Y	Thurs.	Fri.	Sat. W	Sun.
Low energy	3	6	2	5	5	2	3
Insomnia	2	4	3	6	6	3	4
Poor appetite	2	4	2	4	5	3	2
Negative thoughts	2	3	2	4	4	2	3
Negative mood	3	5	2	6	6	3	3
Anxiety	2	6	3	4	5	3	3
Totals	14	28	14	29	31	16	18

Emily created this log in her notebook and put it next to her bed, filling it in every night before going to bed. At the end of the week she added up her numbers to see how the totals reflected on her week. She could see easily from the totals that she generally felt better on the days that she did exercise.

You can create a mindfulness log of this sort in the journal you're using for this book. Tailor it to your individual symptoms. You can add little sentences or notes to yourself as to why some days are particularly difficult or good to help you identify patterns of your depressive symptoms. For example, Emily could write under her log for Friday, "Presentation at work . . . I was anxious," to explain the jump in numbers for that Friday. On Saturday she could note, "I took an extra long walk to work out my tension from the meeting." Over time a log of this sort will help you understand what makes you feel better or worse. It will also give you the chance to identify the feelings in your mind and body that tell you how you are feeling.

Goals of Exercise

Goals will vary from person to person. When you are establishing goals you want to make sure they are specific to you and not so broad that they remain elusive. If you say, "I want to be fit," that alone is a very general and could use more specificity. Make your goals reachable and specific, as you can always create new goals once you have reached your first one. Consider creating a goal that you can stick with and perhaps reach within four weeks. A very reasonable goal would be to just keep going with an exercise program for four weeks, eliminating any concerns about performance. Having a specific time-driven goal helps some people. For example, you may want to start off with being able to walk a mile in under fifteen minutes. If you are a person who is driven by stress and demands, you may not want to create a goal that intensifies this trait, rather you may want to consider exercising mindfully, tuning in to your body, breath, and sensations as you exercise.

Consider the following example. Bob tracked his activities in chapter 3 and noticed he was very depressed at his first work meeting every week. He discovered that he does not schedule anything for himself outside of work, and that his one good day occurred when he got up early and went to the gym before going to work. Using this information, he examined his thoughts before the first work meeting and noticed that he was thinking, "I hate being here—I can't stand doing this all day." He challenged this by saying to himself, "It isn't the worst thing I've ever been through. I don't have to be in this meeting all day, and things usually get better over the course of the day." He then decided to schedule a visit to the gym before work. He worried that he would fail to go to the gym, so he decided to start small. He scheduled visiting the gym just two times the next week (up from one the previous week). Bob started attending the gym two days a week.

When he first went, he hadn't worked out in a while and was unsure what sort of shape he was in. He remembered that in high school he could bench press 150 pounds, and decided that was his goal. When setting up his exercise program, his first thought was, "I should be able to start at 150. It's embarrassing if I can't do that." When he noticed this thought, he realized it fit with his core theme of, "I'm not good enough." Taking a more mindful approach, he told himself, "I don't know how much I can lift right now. I really want to be able to lift like I used to, but that may not be realistic. If I can't lift 150 right now, I will still survive." He then decided to start doing repetitions with fifty pounds to get started, and to increase weight at ten pound increments as he felt comfortable. In doing the lifts, he practiced being mindful, noticing both the physical sensations of the lifting as well as the self-critical thoughts that passed by when he was lifting low weight.

By noticing the interfering thoughts, Bob was able to address them and then develop a step-by-step plan to move him on his way to achieving his goal.

Yoga as Mindfulness

Yoga can be a wonderful means of putting mindfulness into practice while simultaneously getting the benefits of exercise. Stretching, bending, flexing, extending, and holding the body in many different poses cajoles the mind into being centered in the body and out of depressive thinking. Yoga poses are so demanding that you cannot be preoccupied with depressive thoughts and yoga at the same time. Yoga requires you to be fully present in your body while you keep your balance in challenging positions or stretch beyond what you thought was possible. It's impossible to be present and balanced in your body if your mind is in the swirl of a depressive thought pattern. In other words, the concentration needed to do yoga safely can draw the mind away from negative thinking.

At the same time that the negative thoughts are transformed by the demands of yoga, the direct experience of putting your body into different positions changes the energy of your body. Your body is opened by the yoga positions, by your breath, and by your expanded awareness. Yoga can give you the chance to become conscious of the different parts of your body by directing your awareness and attention to these body parts. As you breathe into your body, you can feel the place where the body is restricted softening with the breath and relaxing with the attention. You can realize that expansion can happen in your body, as well as your mind.

For people who are struggling with depression, the poses that are usually recommended are ones that open the chest. Imagine what a depressed person looks like. For most people, the image of depression is of someone with their head down, chest collapsed, shoulders rounded and hunched, and eyes downcast. Yoga poses to relieve depression are designed to uncurl this depressed body and breathe life into it. Patricia Walden, a nationally recognized yoga teacher, provides some suggestions about doing yoga if you are depressed. She recommends keeping your eyes open so you don't drop back into your depressive thoughts. Walden recommends a different variation of poses according to the type of depression the yoga student is experiencing. For the depressed person who is lacking energy and combating fatigue, she recommends supported back bends and inversions (where you are in some version of being upside down), poses that typically uncurl the compressed oxygen-deprived chest, typical of the depressed person's posture. For people who are more anxious she suggests a more active sequence of postures that get the heart rate up and also open the chest so people can breathe more deeply (Walden 1999).

It is beyond the scope of this book to go through all the poses available for the treatment of depression. If you choose to pursue yoga as an activity, we advise that you seek the guidance of a qualified yoga teacher, as well as study books on the practice of yoga.

A Note from Paula

I have been practicing yoga now for nine years, attending classes on a regular basis in the style of yoga founded by B.K.S. Iyengar. Yoga is a challenging and gratifying way to transform my mindfulness meditation practice into a physical expression. The spiritual and emotional gifts of yoga seem to be linked to the physical demands of yoga as I need to stay focused in the present moment to do the poses of yoga. Over time many of the poses are remembered in my body; it is like visiting an old friend each time I practice. Like a friend whose years of familiarity gives you comfort, the familiar poses give me a connection to myself. But part of the challenge of yoga is not just dropping into this familiar relationship, this pose that I have done hundreds of time, but instead reaching for new capacities and new connections to my body. On a practical note it is great to come to a yoga practice and let go of the worries of the day, while feeling my attention penetrating in and through my body. I frequently have the experience of going to a yoga class at the end of a grueling day, feeling tired and drained, and leaving the class feeling happy and content.

But the practice is not always sweet or easy. On many occasions I have been gripped with fear while doing yoga. During these moments I fall back on my practice of meditation to remind myself to just stay with the moment, stay with the body, and let nonjudgmental awareness guide me as I stay with my fear, and move further into my body. These moments feel as though some aspect of my core beliefs has been physically activated, and presented to me. Like the practice of mindfulness meditation, the practice of yoga allows me to notice my thoughts and fears, and feel the associated contractions in my body. At times I can move into and through the contraction and feel better, and other times the contraction remains there, but is usually softer, less dense, and less feared. I know I'll be able to visit the tension again and learn something beyond the wisdom of words by that visitation. Overall, I am very grateful to have a physical exercise, a physical practice, which both helps me feel good and teaches me so much.

A Regular Routine

Making a regular routine of exercise can be extremely helpful with depression as well as general health maintenance. There are few things that you can do that can give you so much in return with so few drawbacks. Given this, consider engaging in an exercise program that is pleasing to you and perhaps even fun! You don't have to make yourself miserable to get the benefits from exercise. Start off with some exercise you can maintain and begin to monitor your shifts in mood. Good luck!

10

acceptance is not defeat

Many situations in life are persistent, no matter how much we want them to change. Depression often results from the frustration over unchanged and unwanted situations or states of mind. Learning how to effectively cope with what is unchanged and unwanted can move you out of a depressed state of mind into a more neutral, flexible, and even content state of mind. In this chapter we will explore how to use mindfulness and CBT to nurture acceptance and explore how acceptance is change and not defeat. We will discuss how shifting your mental attention helps you move towards acceptance of life.

The Benefit of Acceptance

It sounds so very nice to drop the ego and just be with life as it unfolds moment by moment. But most of us really want some aspect of our life situation or personality to change before we believe we can be happy. However, after months or years of persistent effort towards change, you may notice that despite all your hopefulness and or hard work that some things just haven't changed. Or perhaps you married your spouse with the idea that because he or she loved you they would certainly make the effort to change an irritating personality characteristic, and somehow this has yet to occur, even after your years of efforts to help them make the change!

The concept of cultivating acceptance is reaching a wider range of recognition among researchers and therapists as an important strategy for working with very difficult psychological and physical problems. This is true not only in the treatment of depression but also in couple's therapy and treatment of patients with chronic pain, schizophrenia, and borderline personality disorder. Broadly speaking, what researchers have found is that efforts to avoid thoughts and sensations associated with the problem often exacerbate the very issue people are trying to resolve. Research has shown that when people try to avoid certain situations or memories, over time their avoidance efforts tend to become associated with the very thing the person is trying to avoid. For example, let's say that you're depressed because you broke up with your spouse. To cope, you make efforts not to think about things you did with your spouse, the places you went together, and the fun times you shared. As you try your best to avoid these memories, new problems are created because now you have people and places that need to be avoided. Sadly, you have created a life of constriction. What acceptance theory suggests is to acknowledge your loss, your anger, your sadness, and to learn to stay with those feelings so ultimately you don't have to avoid them. As Marc Epstein puts it in his book, *Going to Pieces without Falling Apart,* "We don't have to cure every neurosis, we just have to learn how not to be caught by them" (1999, 119). But how do we prevent getting caught up in self-defeating thoughts, much less intense depression? To move in this direction is to learn to expand your attention, both internally and externally. We find this ability to shift attention to be extremely valuable to the patients we see who are depressed, in pain, and even psychotic. When people are able to do this, we let them know they are using a teaching tool that Charlotte Joko Beck has long called the Big Container.

The Big Container

Successful movement out of depression occurs when people enlarge their container of self-awareness. In dialectical behavioral therapy, a cognitive therapy model that addresses acceptance, you neither avoid misery nor focus exclusively on your misery, but rather track your misery levels on a daily basis *and* turn your attention towards skills that can make you feel less miserable. This inclusive approach of tracking moods and making sure the awareness container is getting larger is rooted in the practice of mindfulness meditation.

Indeed, this very practice teaches us how to be open to our mental and or physical anguish, and be aware of the greater container of our life, such as the space we are sitting in, the sound of the breeze, and the sensation of the air on our cheek. There is a delicate balance between being aware of mental and physical tension and indulging that tension. The balance is often tipped towards indulgence when we forget that we live in a broad container, notably this whole world. This is one reason why there is such emphasis on maintaining an awareness of your surroundings while meditating. To stay firmly planted in reality, you notice and label the thoughts that arise and note the ever-changing physical sensations in your body, while maintaining an awareness of where your body contacts the surface on which you sit.

You might ask how you can maintain this broad and open awareness in your everyday life, especially when you are feeling downright depressed and grumpy. With experience you can learn how to tolerate or *be* with these difficult moments. At first it is helpful to practice these skills when you feel slightly low so that the skills are accessible to you when you feel moderately down or even very blue. Once the skills become easily available you can start to integrate them into your everyday life.

You might wonder how someone who is very depressed gets motivated to shift their attention to the big container. Frank was working as a midlevel sales manager when he had his first episode of major depression. The depression was worsened by the lack of promotions in this job. He was passed up because of his tendency to get angry and lose his temper both with his supervisors and occasionally with his customers. Frank became so preoccupied with his anger at his supervisors that he briefly considered killing them and then turning the gun on himself. Fortunately, this notion frightened him, and he sought admission into a hospital. We treated Frank as an outpatient the year after his admission. At this time he was no longer working in the same job, thus was relieved of anger so severe it prompted murderous and suicidal thoughts. As you might imagine, however, he was still often angry. Frank came to acknowledge that his anger was a very big problem. He began to see how he used anger to avoid feeling tender or vulnerable. Thus his container of awareness grew larger when he started to tune into what he was avoiding. He started meditating every day for about five minutes a day. He lived in a grimy apartment, so he tried to do his meditating away from the apartment. Sometimes he did it in a nearby park, where he took the time to carefully observe the birds flitting to and from the trees. One day he described helping an old man carry a box home from the post office. He was surprised that this old gentleman wasn't afraid of him and didn't think that Frank was going to take off with the box. In telling the story, Frank was stirred up and close to crying—a big shift for this burly tough guy. Frank's container of awareness had expanded beyond his anger as he began to experience tenderness in his everyday life.

Shifting Your Lens of Awareness

Mental and physical training in maintaining a broad awareness is critical when treating depression. Picture depression as measuring scales being tipped towards negative self-absorption. If the mind has no way to shift its focus, then depression will naturally continue. Mindfulness training does not ask the client to avoid the stimuli that contribute to the depression, but to learn to broaden their awareness so that these stimuli shift from the foreground to the background. Attention can be focused like a camera lens. The shift from foreground to background happens when we refocus our internal camera lens on the big picture rather than on the specific target of our misery. The lens of our awareness sees the misery but is no longer using the close-up lens to focus exclusively on it; rather the close-up lens has been exchanged for a wide-angle lens that can include both the foreground and the background. With this change in focus the misery can be viewed in context, like one object in a broad landscape, more neutrally and potentially with less harsh judgment. Compassion can arise from the heart when we view the conditions of our life in a neutral frame.

This acceptance of life as it is doesn't happen overnight. But you move in the direction of acceptance as you develop the mental willingness and physical capacity to experience each moment as it is in a nonjudgmental fashion. Learning to watch the mind and recognize harsh self-judgments, you begin to see these self-critical thoughts as red neon lights blinking out warning signs as to how you are rejecting yourself and life. As you become willing to notice the harsh thoughts that run through your mind, you increasingly recognize them as simply an activity of your mind. As you become aware that these harsh thoughts are not necessarily even accurate or real you take an important step towards acceptance.

It's important to understand that acceptance does not mean resignation or even liking the situation. Rather it means having the willingness to be with all aspects of the self, knowing full well that there are aspects of our personality or our life situation that we want desperately to change. Acceptance work is fostered both when you are working on clearly seeing and being with a part of yourself, as well as being willing to hang in there as best you can with an external situation that you cannot change. Instead of just focusing on how much you dislike a characteristic way of thinking or situation (either internal or external), acceptance work asks you to observe and be willing to physically feel the sensations in the body, both those that are loved and loathed. These aspects of our self are observed by the mind and experienced in the body over and over again. But, while these parts of our personality may or may not change in fundamental ways, our *relationship* to these aspects of our personality can shift in a positive direction. Because we allow ourselves to stay with the physical sensations in the body, the avoidance of the loathed aspects of the self diminishes. We learn in the body how to endure the seemingly unendurable. We learn in the mind how to be less reactive to what was previously painful. Over time what flowers from this acceptance work is the capacity to have more tender heartedness, more compassion for the conditions of our suffering.

Frank moved toward acceptance by seeing that under his anger there was often the fear of being rejected by others. He learned to tolerate this fear of rejection, to feel his heart thump and his desire to lash out or beat a quick retreat. Tolerance of painful emotions has been a crucial stepping-stone for Frank in his battle against depression. As we will discuss further, distress tolerance is the dance between allowing the presence of painful feelings and shifting our lens of awareness so that painful emotions do not obliterate our world, our vision, and cause us to be lost in the world of depression.

Distress Tolerance

Marsha Linehan, Ph.D. has coined the term "distress tolerance" when describing a set of skills based on accepting the moment and opening the lens of awareness so that a manageable reality is in the foreground and misery is in the background. On the surface it seems ironic to suggest that skills that shift your attention away from the stressful agent are part of an acceptance strategy. But you must understand that before you do this shifting of attention, you use your lens of awareness to acknowledge that you feel crummy and then consider other ways of managing your stress in this moment. It's not an avoidance of the problem—it is including the problem and moving on. Dr. Linehan defines distress tolerance as "the ability to perceive one's environment without putting demands on it to be different; to experience one's current emotional state without attempting to change it; and to observe one's own thoughts and action patterns without attempting to stop or control them" (1993, 96). What we see in our clients who do the work of distress tolerance is that the acceptance of distress and real-life difficulties leads to changes in other behaviors and thoughts. Through self-awareness they learn the disadvantages of avoiding life through substance abuse, overeating, and overworking, or any number of other available strategies to avoid feeling the gunk of life.

When we teach clients to tolerate the suffering in their lives, we make it clear that toleration is not the same as liking or approving of the difficult life situation. It's important to have a foundation in mindfulness practice, and particularly nonjudgmental observation of emotions, thoughts, sensations, and behavioral patterns before jumping into distress-tolerance skills. This foundation is important because it is through mindfulness that you develop the familiarity of paying attention moment by moment to what you are experiencing in your life. Once you start to deeply pay attention to your every-day life, you are not turning away from life—rather you are beginning to see the whole truth of your life. Linehan uses the term "radical acceptance" to suggest that "freedom from suffering requires acceptance from deep within of what is" (1993, 176). This acceptance does not mean that you are happy about what is going on. It does mean, however, that you are willing to both recognize the distress of your circumstances and use distress-tolerance tools to manage your life when you're miserable. It is as if you are saying to yourself, "Yes, I'm feeling pretty rotten. I can choose to do some things to help me deal with the fact that I'm feeling so bad." You are not saying to yourself, "I am so screwed up because I feel so miserable and I can't stand it anymore and I have to get out of here." The mindfulness attitude is one of acknowledging the misery and moving the mind to help hold the misery in a larger and quite possibly more pleasant and compassionate field of awareness.

Before we describe the varying distress tolerance skills we want to caution you to use them judiciously. Distress tolerance skills are not to be implemented the first time you feel mildly unhappy or distressed. Why is that? Well, because you have a host of mindfulness and CBT skills that you have learned thus far that can be of help to you. Furthermore, distress tolerance skills are based on the notion that acceptance of life is ultimately far more transformative than the avoidance of life.

Dr. Segal, a prominent researcher in mindfulness and depression, shared in a conversation a curious phenomena that he has observed in patients who had overused a three-minute breathing space (which is further discussed in chapter 11). What he found is that the patients who turned to their breath every time they became anxious or stressed ended up having higher rates of relapse into depression. He speculated that rather than mindfulness skills, they were developing avoidance skills, and this ultimately made them vulnerable to depression. This cautionary story is not to say don't use distress tolerance skills, but use them mindfully and develop a repertoire of skills, so when life is very difficult you have a way of turning your attention to ease your pain.

Distraction

Distraction is one of the techniques you can use to tolerate the distress you are experiencing. It is a fairly natural technique, one that you've probably used in the past to change your mood. For example, have you ever noticed that you were in a lousy mood and you decided to watch a funny movie on TV? This is a distraction technique. You are engaging in some sort of activity to change your mood, push away negative thoughts, and to engage in an emotion that is different from sadness.

Distraction is accomplished when you turn your attention away from the things that are making you feel bad. Distraction can be done quietly, without any overt change in behavior. You simply have to push away the thoughts that are making you feel bad and make yourself think about more neutral or pleasant situations. This is where the phrase, "I'm going to put it on the back burner," comes into play. You know the troublesome issue is there, but you're choosing to let it go for the time being. A different distraction strategy occurs when you engage your body, your field of sensations, in a change. For example, taking a shower or listening to music can be a great distraction technique.

Another very helpful technique is acting in a fashion that is opposite to how you are feeling. (Linehan uses this strategy for both distress tolerance and emotion regulation. Elements of both are synthesized in this explanation.) "Opposite emotion" only works when the emotion is not appropriate to the situation. For instance, imagine that you are feeling anxious and nervous because you're walking in a dangerous section of town. In this situation, anxiety may be perfectly appropriate; it may give you a useful degree of vigilance as you walk the city streets. However, if you're feeling anxious and nervous when you wake up in the morning and have nothing more than your usual nonthreatening day facing you, anxiety may not be necessary. When the emotion doesn't suit the situation, you may want to try to act in a way that is opposite to the emotion. For example, let's say you wake and notice that your face is tense, eyebrows furrowed, and your stomach is churning. You decide you are going to try to act in a way that is opposite to your emotion. You put on some of your favorite rock n' roll music and sing loudly and dance for five minutes. The dancing and singing help you breath deeply, helps your face relax, and essentially changes the brain and body chemistry that was previously in place. Even the fact that you are doing something goofy is opposite to the anxiety you were just experiencing.

Distraction can be seen as a continuum where first the mind shifts its attention to something else, and second, the body is engaged to make you feel different. In the above example, the first distraction technique after you notice the tension is to tell yourself that you are going to focus your thoughts on other things. If this doesn't work, you may think about "contributing," another distraction technique where you try to do something beneficial for someone else. Now you are not only distracting yourself through your thinking, but you added a behavior that further distracts you from your anxiety.

Self-Soothing

Eyes, ears, nose, tongue, and skin: These are the five sense organs that are the pathways for soothing the mind and body. Consider what you like to look at, hear, smell, taste, and feel, and you can start to develop a list of distraction techniques to use for each of the senses. Are you a person who is thrilled to listen to a new piece of music, or is a tasty meal what most pleases your senses? Or perhaps you're a person who likes nothing better than having a pair of confident hands giving you a deep massage. Knowing effective self-soothing strategies before you are in a very distressing spot can help short-circuit stressful situations ahead of time.

A benefit of mindfulness practice is that when you learn to pay attention to each moment, you start to notice small, everyday events. You taste that first sip of coffee mindfully, noticing the aroma, the warmth of the cup in your hand, the liquid slipping from your mouth down your throat and into your stomach. Mindfulness can wake you up to your senses, and this awakening can be used to paradoxically help you accept your state of mind and distract you from your previously distressed state of mind.

Improving the Moment

Sometimes in life there are situations that cannot be shifted in a fundamental sense, but there *are* ways you can improve aspects of the situation by taking care of yourself in the midst of the distress. Toleration of stress comes with having a treasure chest of good self-care skills. Self-care skills are not new. They are written about in many books crowding the self-help aisles of bookstores around the world. What makes self-care effective is knowing which self-care skills work for you. To know what is effective you must try different skills and determine which ones work best. You can use the CBT model to rate their effectiveness, helping you figure out what self-care skills you find useful. For example, in dialectical behavioral therapy classes we have people rate, on a 1 to 10 scale, how effective it was to use different skills. You can also conduct experiments, like we described in chapter 6.

Imagery

Many people have found that bringing to mind a pleasant scene or image can help them better tolerate difficult moments. You can imagine yourself in a lovely place; say at a sandy beach where the glimmer of the setting sun bounces rays of light off the water. In your mind's eye you can see the sunset and enjoy the feeling of relaxation, letting your mind dance in the waves. Imagery can be very helpful to use in times of distress. If using an image doesn't work for you at first, try the strategy again using a different image. Remember that using imagery for self-soothing is a skill. Like other skills, it can be learned and improved through practice. One of our clients used imagery to deal with a noisy neighbor in an apartment complex. The neighbor played music loudly, music the client didn't like. Even after many attempts to talk with the neighbor, the music continued—as did our client's increasing stress level. She decided to erect a mental sound barrier between she and her noisy neighbor. This barrier empowered her and enabled her to focus on activities at home without persistently paying exclusive attention to the unpleasant music. Her self-esteem increased as she was successfully able to use this imagery to improve her moment. Some people get discouraged trying to use imagery if their image is not as clear as what they see with their eyes open. Don't worry about this; your image doesn't have to be very exact. You can explore if it works better for you to have more or less detail in your image.

Meaning

When life is very difficult, you can improve the moment by finding the meaning or the lesson in challenges you are going through. One way to find meaning in difficult life experiences is to acknowledge to yourself that you are deepening as a person by accepting reality and learning to cope with it. It often takes heartache to open the heart. And when the heart opens, the tenderness can help us remember that there is meaning to heartache. Difficult times often draw people closer together, and this can help people find meaning in tough situations.

Prayer

Prayer is another means of opening your heart and finding the strength to continue. Naturally, prayer will vary from person to person, religion to religion, and culture to culture. Consider how you might be comfortable praying, and what sort of help or inner guidance would be genuinely useful.

Relaxation

The moment is often improved by relaxing the body. This can often be jump-started by remembering to simply breathe. Just taking a few minutes out to consciously breathe a few breaths is a big help for most people. Most people have a picture in their mind of what is personally relaxing. Certainly whatever means you have for relaxing the body should be cultivated, as this will certainly help you improve the moment and even enjoy it.

One Thing in the Moment

Doing one thing at a time can help reduce stress because you are reducing the number of things that you're trying to accomplish in a moment. Instead, you can try to keep your entire attention on one activity. Essentially this is a mindfulness practice, where you engage your mind and body in what you are doing at this moment. There is no magical activity for successfully doing one thing in the moment, but as with other distress tolerance skills, it is useful to have practiced them before you are in the midst of an extremely distressing event.

Taking a Vacation

You can improve your moment by taking a brief vacation from the situation. For example, getting a magazine that you don't normally read and letting yourself spend thirty minutes thumbing through the pages, or making some yummy chocolate milk and curling up with a blanket and drinking it down. Recently Paula decided to practice taking a vacation at home by laying under a tree for an hour, something she loves to do but has rarely done in her own back yard.

Encouragement

Have you been to football or baseball games and heard the crowd scream, "Go, go, go!" Well sometimes we need to give ourselves words of encouragement to keep going! You can be your own cheerleader, or say simple sentences to get you through tough times. Think about what words or phrases you might find useful when you are in a difficult situation.

Guided Meditation

Following is a guided meditation on acceptance. This meditation is here for you to use as guidance through reading, practicing, and even making your own recording. Often it is very helpful to actually make a recording for yourself of what is written, as it will help you to hear yourself speak the words, which in itself can be very powerful. Furthermore, a recording provides a ready structure to follow, helping the mind to relax as it follows the guidance, rather than trying to remember what to do next. We encourage you to make your own recording so that you can use it for as long as you need.

The following meditation on acceptance is inspired by San Diego Zen Center teacher Elizabeth Hamilton's guided meditations.

A Meditation on Acceptance

Allow yourself to sit in a relaxed fashion, with your back supported, the crown of your head gently lifted toward the sky, and your feet placed as though they were rooted in the ground. Let your eyes close and your body settle down. Allow the tension in your body to ease. Become aware of the sensations of the breath moving in and out.

Allow your mind to turn toward an area of worry, distress, or something that makes you feel depressed. As best as you're able, permit yourself to fully feel this point of worry, noticing the thoughts that arise or any images that come to mind. Let yourself feel the worst part of the situation. Notice how your body is feeling now. Be aware of any sensations as they come and go. There is no need to try to change any sensations. Simply recognize whatever sensations or emotions arise. Stay with these sensations and emotions for a few moments.

Now allow your attention to return to your breath, feeling the flow of your breath into the body and the flow of the breath leaving the body. Feel your belly inflate and deflate. Now let your mind return to the area of worry or discomfort. Allow the breath to move into the sensations of discomfort, providing air to cushion and permeate the concerns.

As you feel the breath move into and mix with the unpleasant thoughts and sensations, you can either place your attention back and forth between the breath and the unpleasant sensations or maintain simultaneous awareness of both the breath and the unpleasant sensation. If the unpleasant sensations are changing, just allow the change to occur. You don't need to try to hold on to the discomfort, and you don't need to try to make the discomfort go away. Do this for a few rounds of your breath.

As you continue breathing and paying attention to the sensations in your body, allow yourself to include hearing sounds. Pay attention to the sounds that are closest to you, and then let yourself to pay attention to sounds that are subtle. Hear the sounds that are both near and far. Feel the vibrations of the sounds as they arrive in your ears.

Now allow your container of awareness to widen, including the larger space, the sounds, the feeling of air against your body, the warmth or the coolness of the room. Continue to feel the sensations of distress. Hear the sounds, feel the sensations, and feel the tide of your breath move in and out. Let your awareness be broad, feeling everything that can be felt and sensed, and just letting them all be experienced at this time.

In a recent newsletter at the Zen Center of San Diego there was a quote from Charlotte Joko Beck, the senior teacher at the center. She wrote, "Life is a series of endless disappointments, and it's wonderful just because it doesn't give us what we want. Instead of fighting and struggling with disappointment, the key is to rest willingly in it. This may sound forbidding; yet the people who endlessly practice are the ones who eventually know what joy is. I'm not talking about endless happiness (there's no such thing), but joy." This quote speaks to the heart of this chapter on realizing that acceptance is not defeat. For it is with radical acceptance of your depression that you can transform your life, perhaps using the tools of mindfulness and CBT to let the opportunity of depression unfold, like a flower opening to the light of day.

As we move into the final chapter of this book, "Stages of Change," please consider using the elements of radical acceptance to clearly see where you are right now in terms of coping with depression, so you can best use this model to help you identify where you are in the change process.

11

stages of change

Now that you've come this far in understanding some of the philosophy and skills from mindfulness practice and CBT, we want to help you understand where you are now in the stages of changing your behavior. The goal of this chapter is to help you assess and come to terms with the nature of the change process itself and to help you consider how to move forward in that process to improve what is problematic in your life and to build on what is positive.

A Model for Change

We all know that change doesn't come easily and that it's easy to slip back into old, unhealthy behaviors. As we have discussed sometimes it is wiser to come to terms with what is unchangeable, and other times it's healthier to recognize what is holding us back from realizing our true potential. Sometimes we don't go for the gold, our true potential, because we haven't really done the necessary backup work to support the new changed behavior. James Prochaska, John Norcross, and Carlo DiClemente are psychologists who have done extensive research on how to make effective self-change (1994). They have identified specific stages of change that each person goes through as they overcome their problem. What's encouraging about this model of change is that it lets you identify exactly where you are in the change process. You then have a better notion of the appropriate skills to be implemented at that stage to help you have successful movement to the next stage of change. This model has been used to help people unravel their depression, as well as change problematic behaviors like addiction to cigarettes, alcohol, and overeating. It has helped people work through their problems without the aid of therapy or change groups.

What this group of psychologists argue is that there are six stages of change that can be identified across a variety of problems, and that at each stage there are specific tasks to be completed to be able to move to the next stage. We will look at the stages of change and how you can implement the skills from CBT and mindfulness to help you work toward you ultimate goal of developing a more satisfying life.

The six stages of change are:

✦ Precontemplation

✦ Contemplation

✦ Preparation

✦ Action

✦ Maintenance

✦ Termination

Precontemplation

Before you can change a problem you have to recognize that you have one. Precontemplators generally fall into two groups when it comes to people who are depressed. They may fall into the classic definition of precontemplation as a group of people who resist acknowledging they have a problem (as is often the case with people who have a problem with addiction). You may know a person who falls into the classic definition of precontemplation, or you may recognize some of the qualities in yourself. Typically the friends and family around someone in the precontemplation stage recognize the problem before the person fully acknowledges to himself or herself that it's there. It could be the mother's concern over the adolescent daughter who doesn't want to see her friends but can't say why, or the coworker who is aware that their colleague is depressed, drinking too much every night, and not performing effectively on the job the next day. People who are in the stage of precontemplation use the defense of denial, where they steadfastly refuse to face their painful thoughts and emotions. Folks in this stage refuse offers of help. While this stage is often painful for people to observe in others, it is helpful to recognize that someone who is in the stage of precontemplation may feel safe in their problem. To confront them and try to get them to change their behavior usually backfires, as they simply are not ready because they haven't yet fully acknowledged they have a problem.

Unlike the precontemplators who are denying they have a problem, many people who are depressed may be in the precontemplation stage simply because they lack knowledge about the symptoms of depression. They realize something is wrong, but they don't understand that what they're suffering from is depression. People who fall into this latter category are likely to get treatment through primary care settings rather than seeking help from mental-health specialists. They may often come to their doctor with problems related to sleep and energy rather than complaints about their sad mood. In fact, more people come to medical doctors than mental health care providers when they are seeking help for their depression.

A common problem for the person in the precontemplation stage is that they rush (or are rushed by family or therapists) into action. They start therapy, only to quit after two sessions, or they take Prozac for a week and then decide that they aren't really depressed and don't really have a problem. These people have not yet fully acknowledged the extent of what's troubling them. When people feel safe in the precontemplation stage, they can then move on to the next stage, contemplation.

Precontemplation Tools

If this precontemplation phase does describe you, some of the tools in this book will be helpful to consider. As we discussed above, it is very hard for someone in the precontemplation stage to acknowledge that there is a problem. Given the difficulty that we all have had at some time in our life in recognizing and changing a problem behavior, a first helpful step is remembering your compassionate heart as you begin to look at your mood problems. Using compassion for yourself in this situation would be like imagining you are a small child who has been hurt and needs care. Compassion is simply recognizing the problem without placing blame for the cause of the problem.

Acknowledging pain, sadness, or despair can be frightening, and it makes perfect sense that you might want to avoid recognizing that these are experiences that speak to you. Another reason to be reluctant to admit that you are depressed would be if you equated depression with being weak or crazy. There can be any number of explanations why you would tend to minimize or deny that there is a problem. If you think you might have a problem but you're not sure, you might consider whether a friend or a family member has spoken to you about their concerns about your behavior. If so, how did you deal with it? Did you listen and look within as they expressed their worry, or did you try to get yourself off the hook by suggesting things weren't so bad or perhaps by thinking that they really had a problem? This would be a time you could review the descriptions of depressive symptoms in chapter 1 and see if they fit your problems.

Bringing nonjudgmental awareness to any stage of change is very helpful, but particularly when you are trying to raise your awareness about a problem mood or behavior. You will benefit from compassion rather than condemnation. Thus we advise you to use mindfulness of your mood and any resistance to change in order to awaken your awareness regarding this stage of working on your depression. Do not try to change your behavior at this point— merely observe what is going on day-by-day, moment-by-moment.

Contemplation

When you move from precontemplation to contemplation you have started to acknowledge a problem and consider diving into its causes and cures. It can either be a time of great growth or great stagnation. You can stagnate in the phase of change if you are chronically contemplative, interested in only analyzing what might be going on but fearful of trying on new behaviors, thoughts, or ways of expressing yourself. On the other hand, when you begin to get a view of the horizon, the contentment of a life without debilitating depression, you may be strongly motivated to look at what is holding you back and consider how to move forward. The perceived benefits of changing your behavior increase as you move from precontemplation to contemplation of change.

If you are reading this book to absorb information but not necessarily try out any of the practices of mindfulness or CBT, you may be in the contemplation stage of change. This is a completely acceptable and healthy place to be, because you must prepare for change before change can be a success. The research done by Prochaska and colleagues has shown that if you try to bypass the precontemplation or contemplation stage and move directly into action it is likely to be unsuccessful. Like the stage of precontemplation, one risk of this stage is doing too much too soon. As with most change, it is accompanied by anxiety. Thus it's important to fertilize your motivation for change by understanding yourself, rather than flying into change only to be greeted by an upsurge of anxiety and defenses.

Contemplation Tools

The contemplation stage is rich with possibilities for integrating mindfulness and CBT. As with the precontemplative stage of change, bringing awareness to your everyday life helps you open up to emotions and thoughts. This can be done through formal mindfulness meditation and less formally by bringing mindfulness to your everyday experiences. Enhanced self-awareness can help you track your shifts in mood from one hour to the next or from one day to the next. In doing this mood tracking you begin to learn about the qualities of your state of mind or the situations that may make you vulnerable to feeling depressed (hopefully without adding negative self-judgments). You are looking at the links in your behavior and thoughts that create depression. Again, at this stage you are not trying to intervene and move out of depression, you are gathering facts. Like Sergeant Friday says in *Dragnet,* "Just the facts, Ma'am!" After your fact-finding adventure you can consider the subtle relationship of these mood shifts to your core beliefs.

For example, Alicia noticed that before her children left for school she was anxious and worried about their welfare. During their school hours she felt uncomfortable and restless. When she dug into these anxious feelings she realized that under the anxiety there were sad and lonely feelings. She came to recognize this - pattern and used this experience to help her move closer to understanding her core belief. She used the downward arrow technique explained in chapter 4 to guide her closer to her core belief. She asked herself, "What is so bad about the children leaving for the school day?" From this question she realized that she was afraid that they wouldn't return home. She further reflected on what it would mean to her if her children didn't return home. She allowed her cognitive defenses to take a back seat as she mindfully and compassionately observed her fear of what life would be like if her children didn't come home. She was able to identify a familiar fear in the pit of her belly that she felt as a child left alone for long hours while her parents worked. When she asked herself what this feeling said to her, she realized that she had felt very vulnerable as a child. These feelings were coming up again now that she was a parent and her kids needed to leave. Alicia had the core belief that she was vulnerable when she was not with a family member.

What Alicia had accomplished in the downward arrow technique is what some therapists would call a "functional analysis," where you examine an event or feeling and remember what preceded the feeling and what followed the feeling. When doing a functional analysis, you try to go back to when the first change in feeling or thought occurred and sort out the function or meaning of each subsequent thought, feeling, or behavior. For example, Alicia recalled a physical sensation of fear and loneliness that was similar to what she felt in her childhood. She was able to make the connection that these sensations of fear and loneliness returned when her children left for school. By understanding that these physical sensations preceded the thought that she was afraid, she was able to work with relaxing both her body and the emotional disturbance that she felt when her children left home. These are the basic tools of cognitive therapy in terms of tracking events and moods, as well as a fundamental observational skill fostered by mindfulness.

It is during the contemplation stage of change that you want to ask yourself how your depression is impacting your family life, personal life, and professional life. This is an excellent time to consider reviewing both the pros and cons of staying like you are right now and the pros and cons of changing. When you do these activities be sure to be as honest as possible about the possibilities so you can understand what you might be afraid of confronting in the next stage of preparing for change. When you feel you are strongly motivated to change, you are then ready to move into the action stage.

Action

If you have reached the action stage you are trying to implement the various strategies that have been described in the preceding chapters. Throughout this book we have attempted to integrate CBT and mindfulness strategies because we believe the blending of these approaches to living offers the best possibility for your action to have a clear vision and a compassionate heart. Now you have a big tool chest to use to inquire within and begin to work on your depression problems.

As you begin the action stage, proceed with care so that you clearly know what you are doing to try to make changes in your life. It is better to make small steps forward using a few strategies for change rather than try to implement a variety of behavior changes at once. Going back to chapter 3 and the goal-setting discussion, remember to make your goals modest and reachable. You didn't get depressed overnight, and it's likely that you won't get free from depression immediately. What is possible, however, is that you can use mindfulness as a foundation for your change. The foundation of a life without incapacitating depression occurs when you can observe your thoughts, feelings, and behaviors with interest and warmth toward yourself. Change occurs not from disliking yourself but by practicing compassion for yourself and others. When you can view your core beliefs and all the manifestations derived from those beliefs with compassion, you have already moved into a change phase. Furthermore, you will have a very strong foundation to turn compassion into action. This action can be both quiet and profound. Quietness comes with a calm mind that can clearly observe your daily life, thoughts, and behaviors. Profound change comes from using your heart of compassion to no longer reject that which cannot be changed, while you move into new thought patterns and behaviors. As you experiment with tracking your activity, mood, and thoughts, and examining what contributes to a pleasant mood versus a miserable mood, you begin the process of integrating CBT and mindfulness. When you challenge yourself with new activities, more people in your life, an exercise program, catching and changing your depressed thinking, improving communication, doing a relaxation program, tolerating distress in your life by turning your attention to other things, and accepting that which is unchangeable, you are using a vast reservoir of action tools.

Action Tools

As we cautioned earlier, when you try to start any new program of change you want to start off with modest goals so you can have success rather then be disappointed with failure. When you make a goal, be sure to consider all the steps that it will take to reach that goal. Each of those steps is a goal in itself, and you can reward yourself at each step of the way! It seems that as adults we are often reluctant to give ourselves rewards, so just notice if you are reluctant to consider a reward system and try it anyway. We often dismiss small changes as easy or meaningless, rather than mindfully noticing, "I am doing something different than I did before." Recognize the thoughts that discount change, then observe and describe change in a nonjudgmental way. Rewards can be scheduling a pleasant event, having time-off, reading a favorite magazine, going to the movies, or walking at your favorite spot. Take the time to make a list of rewards that are meaningful to you and then practice giving them to yourself even when you've made small changes.

Also, when you start trying to change, don't use all the action tools at once because you won't know what is helping you. Remember that your life can be like a fascinating experiment, so be conscious of what change you are implementing and what you are going to use to monitor the effectiveness of that change. In addition, when you are evaluating a new activity or behavior, it's helpful to use a target symptom that is likely to be affected by the new behavior. For example, you might want to evaluate your self-esteem, feelings of pleasure, confidence, etc. on the days you schedule pleasant things to do. To see if these things are useful, evaluate the severity of your target symptoms as a way of monitoring your progress in the action phase.

A surefire way to become disappointed in the action stage is to create unrealistic expectations for relief from depression by doing only one action. Consider Jeff, who had been depressed for a year before he started cognitive therapy. He had scheduled two new activities for the week, and indeed felt better on the days he did the activities. But he felt angry, frustrated, and disappointed that on his nonactivity days he returned to feeling his baseline of depression. He thought, "What is the point of doing anything if my mood doesn't stay good after I stop doing fun things. I'm not really getting better." When Jeff looked at this chain of events with a clear mind he realized that he was discounting that he actually did feel better, and that he'd set his expectations too high. He had expected that two activities would take care of the whole week. From this experience he learned to anticipate change in his depression level on the days he did the activities and not to be disappointed if he felt some depressive symptoms on the days he didn't do scheduled activities. (Naturally, he then had the opportunity to consider what other tools he could use on the days of the week he didn't have scheduled activities to help his mood.)

As you move into making change in your life you will want to consider how to evaluate whether you are making progress toward your goal of becoming less depressed. A tool we use in our cognitive behavioral therapy classes is the Daily Mood Scale* (in appendix). This tool is commonly used on a weekly basis in cognitive-therapy groups to help the client evaluate how they are doing. Consider using this tool in your life on a weekly or monthly basis to help you determine how you are succeeding in this action phase of the treatment of depression.

Besides the Daily Mood Scale, you probably have other ways of knowing whether you are becoming less depressed. You will want to consider what has been the most debilitating aspect of your depression and then watch for changes in those symptoms. As discussed earlier, if you want to figure out if something is working, look at the target symptoms. Using target symptoms can be helpful in both the short-term and long-term analysis of whether a new action is working. Target symptoms can be the common symptoms of depression like: poor energy level, sleep difficulties, feeling blue, appetite changes, irritability, or negative thinking. As you transition from the action phase to the maintenance phase you will want to remember what your target symptoms are because it will be crucial to apply your mindfulness skills to these symptoms when you enter this next phase.

To summarize the action phase of change, there are six steps you can take to get into action:

1. Clearly identify what target symptoms or aspects of your depression you want to change.

2. Make goals modest and attainable.

3. Use mindfulness and CBT tools to reach your goals.

4. Provide healthy and pleasant rewards for your action efforts.

5. Return to your target symptoms to assess whether your action plan has been successful.

6. If target symptoms return, try different mindfulness and CBT skills.

---

* Adapted with permission, Muñoz, R. F., C. Ghosh Ippen, S. Rao, H. L. Le, and E. V. Dwyer. 2000. Manual for Group Cognitive-Behavioral Therapy of Major Depression: A Reality Management Approach. Participant Manual and Instructor's Manual. Available from the author: University of California, San Francisco, Dept. of Psychiatry, San Francisco General Hospital, 1001 Potrero Ave., Ste. 7M, San Francisco, CA 94110.

Maintenance

When you have arrived at the maintenance phase of change you are no longer actively depressed. That is the good news. You have done a lot of hard work to change your lifestyle and thinking habits to get to this stage. But it's not the time to put away your tool chest of CBT and mindfulness skills because you will want them handy to keep from getting depressed again. Prochaska notes that to successfully stay in the maintenance phase two factors are fundamental: "sustained long-term effort and a revised lifestyle" (204).

The integration of CBT and mindfulness is what makes the sustained long-term effort and revised lifestyle possible. The book, *Mindfulness-Based Cognitive Therapy for Depression: A New Approach to Preventing Relapse* describes in great detail how the combination of mindfulness and CBT is especially useful for people who have experienced depression and are now trying to prevent relapsing into another depressive episode (Segal et al. 2002).

Before we move on to discussing how to use CBT and mindfulness strategies to prevent relapse, we want to let you know that there is a serious risk for relapse if you have had a major depression. Zindel Segal, J. Mark Williams, and John Teasdale, the authors of the book mentioned above, have synthesized some of the research regarding relapse. They relate that "recent estimates suggest that at least 50 percent of patients who recover from an initial episode of depression will have at least one subsequent depressive episode, and those patients with a history of two or more past episodes will have a 70-80% likelihood of recurrence in their lives" (pg 14). They go on to describe how many people who have experienced depression can be considered to be vulnerable to a relapse, and indeed may have what constitutes a chronic illness due to the common frequency of relapse. (As described in chapter 1, these people have recurrent major depression.) Thus, given the seriousness of repeated episodes of depression, the authors of the book have devoted considerable research and study to preventing the relapse of depression using CBT and mindfulness. They developed an eight-week class based on many of the principles and practices of the widely used stress-reduction model described by Jon Kabat-Zinn in *Full Catastrophe Living*, a book that has been rightly credited with bringing mindfulness meditation into hospitals, medical clinics, prisons, public schools, and neighborhood community centers. (It was through teaching this model of stress reduction at the VA

Medical Center that the authors of this book first started to collaborate on research.)

Segal and his colleagues have looked at the effectiveness of mindfulness-based cognitive therapy over a period of years. What they discovered when they looked at a group of patients five years after treatment was that the group of patients who had been in the mindfulness-based cognitive therapy program had a 37 percent rate of relapse into depression compared with 66 percent of the control group, who had not learned mindfulness. They began to look at what could contribute to some of the difference and they focused on whether rumination (thinking about your disturbing thoughts over and over) could contribute to future relapses of depression. The mindfulness researchers hypothesized that people practicing mindfulness have learned to bring nonjudgmental awareness to these ruminative thoughts, which gives them some distance from the thoughts and in a sense reduces their emotional influence. Their research has been well-received in the world of psychological research and is now inspiring a new generation of researchers interested in mindfulness and psychology.

Relapse Prevention

Here in California we are advised to have an "earthquake preparedness plan" so that we're prepared in the event of an earthquake. Most people who have lived through an earthquake now have a flashlight by their bed, know how to turn off their gas line, and have a box of emergency supplies on hand. No one would argue against being prepared for an earthquake, and likewise no one should argue that being prepared for another episode of depression isn't also a smart thing to do. It would be very naïve to suggest that once you have read this book and worked through your depression that you will never be sad again. As the Buddha teaches, life by it's inherent nature brings joyful and sad events. Through mindfulness and CBT we can learn to hold these in a compassionate balance.

An important factor in preventing relapse into depression is having your own "early warning system," where you recognize your early signs of depression. Often depression can renew its ugly face with insidious ruminative thinking, an irritable mood, a reluctance to participate in your usual pleasurable events or other symptoms that you may know well. What is imperative is that you know your early warning signs and not ignore them. The temptation will be to ignore the soft signs of depression and tell yourself that they will go away. The signs will go away—when you implement your individualized plan to bring your mood back to normal.

Maintenance Tools

It's best to create your action plan while you're not depressed, because when you are depressed your energy or motivation may be compromised and you may be unable to create a thoughtful plan to help yourself. Segal and colleagues have suggested a four-step plan to use in the face of renewed depressive symptoms. (We are presenting the basics of his plan and incorporating what we have presented in this book.)

1. The first step is to return to your practice of mindfulness and take a "three-minute breathing space." They advise that you use this period of meditation to return to a sense of expanded awareness that will help you put your mood shift into perspective. As we mentioned earlier, when you have practiced mindfulness meditation over time you will have developed a "muscle of awareness." Your breath will guide your muscle of awareness to help you connect to a wider awareness beyond what is distressing to you at this moment, including awareness of your thoughts, physical sensations, and your surroundings. With the aid of mindfulness you can put the factors causing your change in mood into a wider container of awareness.

2. The second step is to do something pleasurable. Hopefully by now you have created for yourself a list of pleasant activities that you like to do. Again, it's important to have made this list while you're not depressed because when you are low it's likely that nothing will seem pleasurable. Hopelessness will make the notion of pleasure seem impossible. So even if you think it's hopeless to try to do something pleasurable, make the effort and do it. As Segal suggests, do something that is "kind to your body," like getting a massage, eating good food, taking a long, hot shower, or any activity that you ordinarily find pleasurable. Again, remember events that you have enjoyed in the past, or things that you have wanted to do but have never done, and get yourself out there doing something!

3. The third step is to do something that gives you a sense of feeling satisfaction, control, mastery, or achievement.

Obviously at different times we will all have different notions of what gives us mastery. Some days it may be getting a letter stamped and in the mail, and other days it might be getting the house cleaned from top to bottom. Whatever you choose, keep in mind that it doesn't have to be complicated and that satisfaction can come in small packages. Keep in mind our advice about breaking down your goals into small steps and congratulating yourself as you reach your goals.

4. The final step is to act mindfully. Now you can focus your attention on to whatever activity you happen to be engaged in and do it with as complete awareness as possible. When you practice mindfulness of daily life, it can be helpful to let yourself slow down and try to accomplish things one step at a time. You may want to tell yourself what you are doing (especially if your mind is moving to negative thoughts) to keep yourself focused on the activity of the moment. For example, you may say to yourself, "Now I'm walking down the hall; now I'm sitting on the couch; now I'm sipping a glass of water." As your mind settles, you can move your attention into the sensations of your activities. The point here is that you try to do whatever you can do to keep yourself focused on the present moment. This process will help you avoid slipping into rumination on negative thoughts.

To summarize, for success in the maintenance phase you must have a personalized sense of how you can keep your depression-fighting efforts going over the long-term, revising your lifestyle to promote balance and joy. From reading this book we hope that you have developed a daily mindfulness practice. There is no right way to have a mindfulness practice other than selecting what you can do regularly and developing a practice that helps you feel connected to a greater whole. For some people it will be taking several three-minute breathing spaces during the day; for others it may be developing a practice of meditating for thirty-minutes every day, or it may be doing yoga regularly. Do whatever has meaning for you. We encourage you to experiment with what works for you so you can use it to maintain your health for a long time.

As important as doing mindfulness will be incorporating what you've learned about CBT to help you develop a revised lifestyle. Consider how your depression started, what made it worse, what type of relationships promoted depression, and what type of relationships helped you feel better. Review what activities you did to help you get out of depression. Also, reflect on the implications of your core beliefs and the automatic thoughts that flow from those core beliefs, and ask yourself whether you know how to work with those automatic thoughts so they don't lead you down the path of depression. Again, we hope that by reading this book you understand how to recognize distorted thinking, challenge thoughts, and work successfully to incorporate a variety of CBT strategies into your daily life.

Termination

The word termination suggests that depression is gone—up and vanished! Everyone knows that it's not possible to have a life without problems, but it is possible to live a life without deep depression. The researchers who identified the six-stages toward successful change suggest that if you are in the termination phases of your problem you have a solid sense of being a person who can handle the problems that previously tore you apart. You have a strong sense of confidence in yourself that comes from working through a problem, inside and out, and personally growing from that struggle. You have adjusted your lifestyle, perhaps with different friends, new activities, and creative approaches to your problem so that you're not vulnerable to what previously made you depressed.

You may know a person who has had many problems in their life, and they are angry and bitter about all of their difficulties. You also may be lucky enough to have encountered people who also have had many tough breaks and unfortunate circumstances but are not basically angry or bitter. Rather, they are grateful for what they have learned from their struggles. They are the ones who remember to be compassionate and mindful toward the anger and bitterness when it arises without becoming identified with it. If you are in the termination phase you may not be grateful for your struggles, but you have undoubtedly developed a lifestyle and coping patterns that prevent you from slipping back into despair. And furthermore, the slippery path back to depression has undoubtedly been tested by life's sorrows, losses, and misfortunes, but your new lifestyle and consolidated coping patterns have weathered these tests. Unquestionably you know yourself well, you know your vulnerabilities, and by now you naturally use your mindfulness and CBT skills to creatively respond to the ups and downs of life.

At this stage of change you are free to move beyond a life defined by depression; you are moving into a life of wellness. You are no longer restricted by the boundaries of depression; rather you can be open to life as it is, able to be with the sorrow and the joy of life, able to realize your deepest potential. When you are open to life moment by moment, a deep healing can occur. And in this healing you can move into a new life beyond the previous constrictions of your defined sense of self. This "you" that you have carried for so long grows smaller, and a connection to all things grows larger. The "you" never quite disappears, for we are conditioned beings, but you can realize a greater capacity to meet life freely.

appendix

Daily Mood Scale						
Day _____						
Mood						
Best	10	10	10	10	10	10
	9	9	9	9	9	9	9
	8	8	8	8	8	8	8
	7	7	7	7	7	7	7
	6	6	6	6	6	6	6
Okay	5	5	5	5	5	5	5
	4	4	4	4	4	4	4
	3	3	3	3	3	3	3
	2	2	2	2	2	2	2
	1	1	1	1	1	1	1
Worst	0	0	0	0	0	0	0

Make photocopies of this form and use it to track your mood.

Automatic Thought Record

Events	Moods	Automatic Thoughts
Who? What? When? Where?	What was your mood in relation to the event? Rate your emotion from, 0-10 0 = worst mood 10 = best mood	Record the most immediate thought that went through your mind when you first noticed your mood. Make an asterisk by the strongest thought.

Photocopy this form and use it to track your automatic thoughts.

Three Cs Form

Where and When:

Feelings (0-100):

CATCH the thought (What I told myself)	CHECK It (What's wrong with this thought)	CHANGE It (What would be a better thought)

Make copies of this form to help you catch and change unhelpful thoughts.

resources

There are a number of other helpful books and Web sites that you may want to use.

Feeling Good (1980) and the *Feeling Good Handbook* (1989) by David Burns are two books that provide a variety of well-explained ways for coping with depression and other problems.

Control your Depression (1978) by Peter Lewinsohn, Ricardo Muñoz, Mary Ann Youngren, and Antonette Zeiss is an excellent book that particularly emphasizes the role of pleasant activities and social support in treating depression.

Thoughts and Feelings (1997) by Matthew McKay, Martha Davis, and Patrick Fanning is a general workbook that provides lots of great exercises for changing your thoughts and activities and to help you better understand your core beliefs.

The Depression Workbook, Second Edition (2001) by Mary Ellen Copeland also provides lots of exercises that are designed for treating depression. A great thing about this book is it also addresses the issue of bipolar disorder (manic depression) and has exercises to help with mania and stabilizing mood, in addition to reducing depression.

Nothing Special: Living Zen (1993) and *Everyday Zen: Love and Work* (1989) by Charlotte Joko Beck are two books that are inspirational, not because they try to be, but because they explain the nuts and bolts of meditation practice with a straightforward style.

Being Zen: Bringing Meditation to Life (2002) by Ezra Bayda is a clearly written book that brings mindfulness to the dilemmas of everyday life.

The Path with Heart: A Guide Through the Perils and Promises of Spiritual Life (1993) by Jack Kornfield is a delightful mix of stories, practical guided meditations, and sensitive explanations on how to seek a spiritual life.

Full Catastrophe Living (1990) by Jon Kabat-Zinn is the classic book that has spearheaded stress-reduction programs around the world.

www.umassmed.edu/cfm is a very helpful Web site for learning more about the Center for Mindfulness. From this Web site you can access places in the country where mindfulness-based stress reduction classes are available, as well as purchase body scan tapes or Cds.

Referral Sources

The following web links can be useful for getting information about treatment.

Aabt.org is the Web site of the Association for Advancement of Behavior Therapy. If you select "find a therapist" you can search for a cognitive-behavioral therapist in a community near you.

AcademyofCT.org is the Web site of the Academy of Cognitive Therapy. This is the only organization that certifies therapists as competent in cognitive therapy. You can search for a certified cognitive therapist by selecting "referrals" on the home page.

Depression.org is the Web site of the National Foundation for Depressive Illness. This organization is dedicated to treatment of depression and bipolar disorder. The emphasis of this Web site is on medications, and a phone number is provided for getting referrals for treatment with medications.

references

American Psychiatric Association. 2000. *Diagnostic and Statistical Manual of Mental Disorders, Fourth Edition, Text Revision.* Washington, D.C.: American Psychiatric Association.

Ancoli-Israel, S. 1996. *All I Want is a Good Night's Sleep.* St. Louis, Mo.: Mosby Year Book, Inc.

Artal, M., and C. Sherman. 1998. Exercise against depression. *The Physician and Sportsmedicine* 26(10):55–60,70.

Beck, A. T., A. J. Rush, B. F. Shaw, and G. Emery. 1979. *Cognitive Therapy of Depression.* New York: Guilford Press.

Beck, C. J. 1989. *Everyday Zen: Love and Work.* New York: HarperCollins.

———. 1993. *Nothing Special: Living Zen.* New York: Harper-Collins.

Beck, J. S. 1995. *Cognitive Therapy: Basics and Beyond.* New York: Guilford Press.

Blair, S., N. Goodyear, L. Gibbons, and K. Cooper. 1984. Physical fitness and incidence of hypertension in healthy normotensive men and women. *Journal of American Medical Association* 252(4):487–90.

Blumenthal J., M. Babyak, K. Moore, E. Craighead, S. Herman, P. Khatri, R. Waugh, M. Nepolitano, L. Forman, M. Appelbaum, M. Doraiswarmy, and R. Krishnan. 1999. The effects of exercise training on older patients with major depression. *Archives of Internal Medicine* 159:2349–2356.

Boorstein, S. 1995. *It's Easier than You Think: The Buddhist Way to Happiness.* New York: HarperCollins.

Byrne, A., and D. Byrne. 1993. The effect of exercise on depression, anxiety, and other mood states: a review. *Journal of Psychosomatic Research* 37(6):565–574.

Casper, R. 1993. Exercise and mood. *World Review Nutrition Diet* 71:115-143.

DeRubeis, R. J., and P. Crits-Cristoph. 1998. Empirically supported individual and group psychological treatments for adult mental health problems. *Journal of Consulting and Clinical Psychology* 66:37–52.

Dobson K. S. 1989. A meta-analysis of the efficacy of cognitive therapy for depression. *Journal of Consulting and Clinical Psychology* 57:414–9.

Doyne, E. J., et al. Running versus weight-lifting in the treatment of depression. *Journal of Consulting & Clinical Psychology* 55(1987):748-754

Dunn, A., and R. Dishman. 1991. Exercise and the neurobiology of depression. *Exercise Sport Science Review* 19:41–98.

Elkin, I., T. Shea, J. T. Watkins, S. D. Imber, S. M. Sotsky, J. F. Collins, D. R. Glass, P. A. Pilkonis, W. R. Leber, J. P. Docherty, and M. B. Parloff. 1989. NIMH Treatment of Depression Collaborative Research Program: General effectiveness of treatment. *Archives of General Psychiatry* 46:971–982.

Epstein, M. 1995. *Thoughts without a Thinker: Psychotherapy from a Buddhist Perspective.* New York: Harper Collins.

Fava, G., C. Rafanelli, S. Grandi, and P. Belluardo. 1998. Prevention of recurrent depression with cognitive behavioral therapy: Preliminary findings. *Archives of General Psychiatry* 55:816–820.

Gorman, C. 2002. The science of anxiety. *Time* 159(23):46–53.

Greenberger, D., and C. A. Padesky. 1995. *Mind Over Mood: A Cognitive Therapy Treatment Manual for Clients*. New York: Guilford Press.

Hamilton, E. 2001. *Zenquiry: A Practice Manual*. San Diego, Calif.: M.T. Head Publications, Zen Center of San Diego.

Hollon S. D., R. J. DeRubeis, M. D. Evans, M. J. Wiemer, M. J. Garvey, W. M. Grove, and V. B. Tuason. 1992. Cognitive therapy and pharmacotherapy for depression: Singly and in combination. *Archives of General Psychiatry* 49:774–81.

Jacobson, N., and A. Christensen. 1996. *Integrative Couple Therapy: Promoting Acceptance and Change*. New York: W.W. Norton & Company.

Judd, L. J. 1997. The clinical course of unipolar major depressive disorders. *Archives of General Psychiatry* 54:989–991.

Kabat-Zinn, J. 1990. *Full Catastrophe Living: Using the Wisdom of Your Body and Mind to Face Stress, Pain, and Illness*. New York: Dell Publishing.

Katon W., and H. Schulberg. 1992. Epidemiology of depression in primary care. *General Hospital Psychiatry* 14(4):237–247.

Keller, M. B., J. P. McCullough, D. N. Klein, B. Arnow, D. L. Dunner, A. J. Gelenberg, J. C. Markowitz, C. B. Nemeroff, J. M. Russell, M. E. Thase, M. H. Trivedi, and J. Zajecka. 2000. A comparison of nefazodone, the cognitive behavioral-analysis system of psychotherapy, and their combination for the treatment of chronic depression. *New England Journal of Medicine* 342:462–1470.

Kornfield, J. 1993. *A Path with Heart: A Guide through the Perils and Promises of Spiritual Life*. New York: Bantam Dell Group.

Lee, I., R. Paffenbarger Jr., and C. Hsieh. 1991. Physical activity and the risk of developing colorectal cancer among college alumni. *Journal of the National Cancer Institute* 83(18): 1324–1329.

Linehan, M. M. 1993. *Cognitive-Behavioral Treatment of Borderline Personality Disorder*. New York: The Guilford Press.

———. 1993. *Skills Training Manual for Treating Borderline Personality Disorder*. New York: Guilford Press.

Linehan, M. M., H. E. Armstrong, A. Suarez, and H. H. Heard. 1991. Cognitive-behavioral treatment of chronically parasuicidal borderline patients. *Archives of General Psychiatry* 48:1060–1064.

Mather, A., C. Rodriquez, M. Guthrie, A. McHarg, I. Reid, and M. McMurdo. 2002. Effect of exercise on depressive symptoms in older adults with poorly responsive depressive disorder. *The British Journal of Psychiatry* 180:411–415.

Matinsen E., A. Medhus, and L. Sandvik. 1985. Effect of aerobic exercise on depression: A controlled study. *British Medical Journal (Clinical Research Edition)* 291(6488):109.

Miranda, J., J. J. Gross, J. B. Persons, and J. Hahn. 1998. Mood matters: Negative mood induction activates dysfunctional attitudes in women vulnerable to depression. *Cognitive Therapy and Research* 22:363–376.

Miranda, J., and J. B. Persons. 1988. Dysfunctional attitudes are mood-state dependent. *Journal of Abnormal Psychology* 97:76–79.

Moyer, W. 1993. *Healing and the Mind.* Television Series. Public Broadcasting Service.

Prochaska, J. O., J. C. Norcross, and C. C. DiClemente. 1994. *Changing for Good.* New York: Avon Books, Inc.

Pronk, N., S. Crouse, B. O'Brien, P. Grandjean, R. Lowe, J. Rohack, J. Green, and H. Tolson. 1997 Training intensity, blood lipids, and apolipoproteins in men with high cholesterol. *Journal of Applied Physiology* 82(1):270–277

Ramel, W., and J. R. McQuaid. 2001. *Mindfulness Meditation, Cognitive Flexibility, and Information Processing.* Paper presented to the 109th Annual Convention of the American Psychological Association, San Francisco, Calif.

Rush, A. J., A. T. Beck, M. Kovacs, and S. Hollon. 1977. Comparative efficacy of cognitive therapy and pharmacotherapy in the treatment of depressed patients. *Cognitive Therapy Research* 1:17–37.

Segal, Z. V., M. Gemar, and S. Williams. 1999. Differential cognitive response to a mood challenge following successful cognitive therapy or pharmacotherapy for unipolar depression. *Journal of Abnormal Psychology* 108:3–10.

Segal, Z. V., J. M. Williams, and J. D. Teasdale. 2002. *Mindfulness-Based Cognitive Therapy for Depression.* New York: Guilford Press.

Silva, M., and M. Shyam. 1994. *Yoga: The Iyengar Way*. New York: Alfred A Knopf.

Simons, A. D., G. E. Murphy, and R. D. Wetzel. 1986. Cognitive therapy and pharmacotherapy for depression: Sustained improvement over one year. *Archives of General Psychiatry* 43:43–50.

Singh N., K. Clements, and M. Fiatarnone. 1997. A randomized controlled trial of the effect of exercise on sleep. *Sleep* 20(2):95–101.

Spence J., P. Poon, and P. Dyck. 1997. The effect of physical-activity participation on self concept: A meta analysis. *Journal of Sports Exercise Psychology* 19:S109.

Stahl, S. 2000. *Essential Psychopharmacology*. Cambridge, UK: Cambridge University Press.

Teasdale, J. D., Z. V. Segal, J. M. G. Williams, V. A. Ridgeway, J. M. Soulsby, and M. A. Lau. 2000. Prevention of relapse/recurrence in major depression by mindfulness-based cognitive therapy. *Journal of Consulting and Clinical Psychology* 68:615–623

Walden, P. 1999. Asanas to relieve depression. *Yoga Journal* November/December:45–49.

Weissman, M. M. 1987. Advances in psychiatric epidemiology: Rates and risks for major depression. *American Journal of Public Health* 77:445–451.

Young, J. E. 1990. *Cognitive Therapy of Personality Disorders: A Schema-Focused Approach*. Sarasota, Fla.: Professional Resource Exchange, Inc.

Youngsteadt, S. 2000. The exercise-sleep mystery. *International Journal of Sport Psychology* 30:241–255.

Zeiss, A. M., P. M. Lewinsohn, and R. F. Munoz. 1979. Non-specific improvement effects in depression using interpersonal skills training, pleasant activity schedules, or cognitive training. *Journal of Consulting and Clinical Psychology* 47:427–439.

John McQuaid, Ph.D., is a clinical psychologist specializing in the treatment of stress and depression. He completed a postdoctoral fellowship at the University of California, San Francisco. In 1995, he joined the University of California, San Diego, Psychiatry department and became a staff psychologist at the Veterans Administration San Diego Healthcare System. He is currently associate professor of clinical psychiatry at UCSD, and director of the Cognitive and Behavioral Interventions Program at the VA in San Diego.

Paula E. Carmona R.N., MSN, is a psychiatric clinical nurse specialist at the Department of Veterans Affairs in San Diego. She graduated from Yale University with a Masters of Science in Psychiatric Nursing in 1986. She trained with Jon Kabat-Zinn and implemented a mindfulness-based stress reduction program at the VA in San Diego. She has been a student of Zen since the 1970's and has been practicing with Charlotte Joko Beck, author of *Everyday Zen* and *Nothing Special,* since 1984. She currently has a private psychotherapy practice in San Diego.

Some Other
New Harbinger Titles

Surviving Your Borderline Parent, Item 3287 $14.95

When Anger Hurts, second edition, Item 3449 $16.95

Calming Your Anxious Mind, Item 3384 $12.95

Ending the Depression Cycle, Item 3333 $17.95

Your Surviving Spirit, Item 3570 $18.95

Coping with Anxiety, Item 3201 $10.95

The Agoraphobia Workbook, Item 3236 $19.95

Loving the Self-Absorbed, Item 3546 $14.95

Transforming Anger, Item 352X $10.95

Don't Let Your Emotions Run Your Life, Item 3090 $17.95

Why Can't I Ever Be Good Enough, Item 3147 $13.95

Your Depression Map, Item 3007 $19.95

Successful Problem Solving, Item 3023 $17.95

Working with the Self-Absorbed, Item 2922 $14.95

The Procrastination Workbook, Item 2957 $17.95

Coping with Uncertainty, Item 2965 $11.95

The BDD Workbook, Item 2930 $18.95

You, Your Relationship, and Your ADD, Item 299X $17.95

The Stop Walking on Eggshells Workbook, Item 2760 $18.95

Conquer Your Critical Inner Voice, Item 2876 $15.95

The PTSD Workbook, Item 2825 $17.95

Hypnotize Yourself Out of Pain Now!, Item 2809 $14.95

The Depression Workbook, 2nd edition, Item 268X $19.95

Beating the Senior Blues, Item 2728 $17.95

Call **toll free, 1-800-748-6273,** or log on to our online bookstore at **www.newharbinger.com** to order. Have your Visa or Mastercard number ready. Or send a check for the titles you want to New Harbinger Publications, Inc., 5674 Shattuck Ave., Oakland, CA 94609. Include $4.50 for the first book and 75¢ for each additional book, to cover shipping and handling. (California residents please include appropriate sales tax.) Allow two to five weeks for delivery.

Prices subject to change without notice.